THE BEST

PUB JOKE

BOOK
Ever! 4

THE BEST

PUB JOKE

BOOK

Ever! 4

JOHN MULLET

CARLTON
BOOKS

CONTENTS

Down the Pub

Jokes for
the local

A woman arrives home after a shopping trip, and is horrified to find her husband in bed with a pretty, firm young woman. She is about to storm out of the house, when her husband stops her by saying, "Honey, before you go, at least give me one chance to explain how on earth this happened!" The woman decides that she owes him this much at least, so stops to listen to his story. He begins, "Well, I was driving home in the pouring rain and I saw this poor thing at the bus stop, soaked. There's a bus strike on, so I offered her a lift and it turned out that she was really hungry. So, I brought her home and gave her some of last night's leftovers. I noticed her clothes were shabby so I offered her that jumper you wore once and didn't like and those trousers that don't fit you any more. I noticed her shoes were full of holes, so I gave her a pair of your shoes that you never liked, too. Anyway, so just as she was about to leave she asked me, 'And is there anything else that your wife doesn't use any more?' So here we are!"

✱✱✱✱

There's a bar where all the regulars are really into body-building. The owner is a body-builder and he only employs body-builders as bar staff. The walls are covered in body-builder photos and they are always having body-builder competitions. On the wall behind the bar is a sign that says, "Win €1,000: Beat The Bartender." Written below it are the rules to the competition: "The bartenders are so strong that, after any one of them has squeezed a lemon with his bare hands, nobody can ever squeeze anything else out of it: anyone who can will win the prize." The space around the bar is filled with photos of people who have tried to win the competition but failed. One day a skinny little man walks into the bar and announces that he'd like to try for the prize. It is a Saturday night, the bar is packed and everybody starts to laugh. The guy's head is about the size of the bartender's hand and nobody believes he has a chance. The bartender picks up a lemon and starts to squeeze it. The juice gushes out quickly, but after a few seconds it stops as the man squeezes everything out: juice, pips, pith and even squashed rind. The bartender then hands the lemon to the tiny old man. The man puts his hand around the wizened, almost unrecognizable lemon and starts to squeeze. To the astonishment of everyone present, juice begins to drip from the fruit and before long seven, eight, nine, and then ten full drops have been squeezed! Everyone starts to cheer and the bartender coughs up the money. "That's amazing – really amazing," says the bartender. "Are you a secret body-builder? Are you a martial arts expert? How did you do it?" "Easy enough," says the man, "I work for the Inland Revenue."

✱✱✱✱

A man gets on a plane and is surprised to be seated next to a parrot. He doesn't really say anything but thinks it a bit odd. When the stewardess comes around to see if anyone wants drinks she asks the man. He says that he'd like a cup of coffee and as he says this the parrot squawks, "And get me a whisky on the rocks, bitch!" The stewardess is visibly shaken and walks off. She comes back a few minutes later and hands the parrot his whisky, but she has forgotten the man's coffee. The man points this out and asks again. As he does so, the parrot squawks, "And bring me another whisky on the rocks you slut!" The stewardess goes off again and comes back – again with the parrot's drink but with no coffee for the man. The man is a bit sick of this so he decides to use the parrot's approach. So he barks, "That's twice I've asked you for coffee, you useless cow, what the hell do I have to do to get a friggin' drink around here?" The next thing the man knows he's been picked up by two huge stewards and thrown out of the plane. He has the parrot next to him and, as they both start their plunge to earth, the bird turns to him and says, "Phew-ee, for someone who can't fly, you sure are one gobby bastard!"

✳✳✳✳

A man walks into a bar. He has a monkey with him. The man orders a drink, and while he drinks it the monkey just runs wild around the whole bar, annoying everyone including the man. While the man is drinking, the monkey runs up to the pool table, climbs up a cue, grabs the cueball, sticks it in his mouth and swallows it. The barkeeper walks up to the man and says, "Did you see what your bloody monkey just did?" "No, what did the little prick do this time?" replies the man. "He just swallowed the cueball from my pool table, that's what he just did," says the barkeeper, angrily. "Well, hopefully it'll kill the little bastard because I'm effing sick of him and his little tricks," says the man. He then finishes his drink and leaves. A couple of weeks later the same man enters the bar with the same monkey. He orders the same drink and the monkey runs wild around the whole bar, in the same manner as the previous time. While the man is drinking, the monkey finds some peanuts on a tray on the bar. He picks one up, sticks it up his arse, takes it out again and eats it. The barkeeper finds this disgusting, so he walks up to the man again. "Did you see what your bloody monkey just did?" "No, what did the little prick do this time?" sighs the man. "He just stuck a peanut up his arse, took it out and ate it," says the barkeeper. "Well, what do you expect?" asks the monkey's owner. "Ever since he ate that sodding cueball he has to measure everything first!"

****

A guy walks into a pub and asks for ten tequila shots. "Sorry, mate," the bartender says, "but that's too much for one go." The guy says, "I just found out that my brother is a homosexual and I'm finding it really hard to deal with," so the bartender says that's OK and that he can have his ten shots of tequila. The next day the very same man walks into the same pub and asks for 20 tequila shots. "Sorry, mate," the bartender says, "but that's too much for one go." The guy says, "I just found out that my son is a homosexual and I'm finding it really hard to deal with," so the bartender says that's OK and that he can have his 20 shots of tequila. The next day the very same man walks into the same pub and asks for 30 tequila shots. The bartender, who's had enough, says to him, "What the hell's the matter – doesn't anyone in your house like pussy?" "Oh, yes," the guy replies, "my wife!"

****

A man walks into a bar. He has a frog attached to his forehead. He says to the barman, "I'll have a gin and tonic, please." The barman pours him the drink – all the while looking at the frog – and gives it to the man. "I'm sorry to be so curious, sir, but I was wondering how on earth you ended up with that thing on you?" he asks. Quick as a flash the frog replies, "I don't know; it started out as a wart on my bum five years ago!"

****

An old boy sits down in his local and asks the barman, an old friend, for a drink. The old boy is wearing a big, old-fashioned stovepipe hat, a black jacket and waistcoat, and a false, square beard. The barman serves him a drink and says, "You off to a party tonight, then?" "Yup," says the man, "I've come as my love life." "What are you going on about?" asks the barman. "You look like Abraham Lincoln." "Indeed I do," says the man, "my last four scores were seven years ago!"

****

Two little old ladies are sitting outside their nursing home having a smoke because it's a no-smoking establishment. It begins to rain and one of them pulls out a condom, cuts the end off and puts it over her cigarette, keeping it nice and dry. The other lady asks her what that thing is. "It's a condom," the little old lady replies. "And where do you get them from?" her friend asks. "Any chemist will sell them to you," the lady replies. The next day, the woman's friend goes off to her local chemist and walks up to the counter. "I'd like some condoms, please, young man," she says to the man behind the counter. "Yes, ma'am," he says, giving her a funny look. "Would you like any particular brand?" "Not really," the little old lady replies, "as long as they'll fit a Camel!"

****

It was the last day of nursery school and all the children had bought presents for their teacher, whom they'd never see again. Because it was the last day, the teacher decided to make a game of guessing what the presents were. First of all the sweetshop owner's daughter comes up with a box. It is quite heavy so the teacher shakes it and says, "Is this full of sweets?" "Yes, miss, it is," replies the little girl. Then the flowershop owner's son comes up with a box. It is very light, so the teacher shakes it and says, "Are these flowers?" "Yes, miss, they are," replies the little boy. Then the wine merchant's son comes up with a box. It is very heavy, so the teacher shakes it a little and notices that it is leaking a bit. She touches a drop of the liquid with her finger and tastes it. "Is this full of wine?" she says. "No, miss," comes the reply. So the teacher tries another drop and then says, "Is this full of champagne?" "No, miss," comes the reply. "In that case I give up," says the teacher, "What's in the box?" "A puppy," the boy says.

****

A guy walks into a bar and orders a double whisky – straight. As he begins to drink he reaches into his wallet and pulls out a photograph. He takes a quick peek at it and then puts it back quickly in his wallet. He then finishes his whisky, calls the barman over and orders another. He begins to drink it and, as he does so, he reaches into his wallet and pulls out the photograph again, looks at it and then puts it quickly away. He continues doing this for about an hour. Eventually the barman asks him, "Hey, mate, what's with the photo? I'm not worried by the amount you're drinking, I'd just really like to have a look at the picture – what on earth is it?" The man replies, "It's a photograph of my wife. When she starts to look good, I know it's time to go home!"

****

A man walks into a bar with a really trendy, new shirt on. The bartender is a woman and she says, "Hey, nice shirt. Really suits you. Where d'you get it?" "Oh, René Kent," comes the reply and the woman is impressed. Shortly afterwards, a man walks into the bar with a really trendy, new pair of trousers on. The bartender says, "Hey, nice trousers. Really suit you. Where d'you get them?" "Oh, René Kent," comes the reply and the woman is impressed. Then another man walks into the bar with a really trendy, new pair of shoes on. The bartender says, "Hey, nice shoes. Really suit you. Where d'you get them?" "Oh, René Kent," comes the reply and the woman is impressed. After a while the door to the bar suddenly bursts open and a man dressed only in his underpants runs in. "Who the hell do you think you are?" asks the bartender. "I'm René Kent!" comes the strained reply.

****

Two men are drinking together in the bar on the top floor of the Empire State Building. The first one says to the second, "You know what? I bet you a hundred bucks I can jump out of that window and not hurt myself." "Bullshit – you're on," says the second man and the first man walks over to the window, opens it and jumps out. Two seconds later – whoosh! – and he is thrown back in. The second guy admits that this is incredible but thinks it must be a fluke, so he offers double or nothing if the first guy can somehow do it again. The first guy takes him up on the bet and walks over to the window, opens it and jumps out again. Two seconds later – whoosh! – and he is thrown back in again. The second guy is amazed again, but now he figures that there must be one of those freak gusts of wind that you get around tall buildings. So, he says to the first guy, "How about this, then: double or quits again, but this time I jump out of the window?" "You're on," says the first guy and the second guy walks up to the window, opens it and jumps out. Five seconds later – whoosh! splat! – he is squashed flat, and dead, on the sidewalk, 70 floors below. The barman pours another drink and says to the remaining man, "You can be a real wanker when you've been drinking, Superman!"

****

Four men are sitting in a bar when a guy comes up to them and offers them a bet. He reckons that he can place a pint glass on the bar, 25 feet away, stand behind their table and piss right into – and fill – the pint glass. The men all confer and decide that there's no way this guy can do it. They quickly stump up the £100 that he's offering. The man walks to the bar, places an empty pint glass on it and returns to where the men are. He stands there, drops his trousers and begins to piss. It goes everywhere apart from the pint glass – he doesn't even get close to it and even pisses on the men with whom he's made the bet. They can't help but laugh at his piss-poor effort. When the guy has finished he hands over the £100. One of the men turns and asks him, "What the hell made you think you could fill that glass all the way over there?" "I never thought I could," said the guy, "but I bet the bartender £500 that I could piss all over you blokes and you'd just laugh about it!"

****

A drunken bum has collapsed on the corner of the street. A policeman comes up to him and asks him what he's up to. "Well," the bum says, "apparently the world rotates on a 24-hour cycle, so I'm waiting for my house to come by. I don't think it'll be long, though,, because I saw my neighbour not so long ago!"

****

A man walks into a bar and sits down for a beer. Now, this guy likes his beer, so when he sees a sign behind the bar that claims, "A lifetime's free beer for he or she who can pass the test," he starts thinking this could be his lucky day. When the owner of the bar comes in, the man says to him, "So what's this about some test, then?" The owner says, "Well, I'll tell you this much: many have tried and many have failed my test and to this day none has passed! It consists of three parts. The first part is simple: just drink one whole gallon of pure jalapeño-laden tequila in one go, without shuddering or uttering a noise. The second part is a little more difficult: there's a vicious croc outside – a pet of mine – and he's got a sore tooth. You have to wrestle him unconscious and get that tooth out using only your bare hands! The third part is tough, too: there's a woman upstairs who hasn't had an orgasm in her 70 years on this earth, and you have to make her come! Complete the three and you will drink free beer in this bar to the end of your days!" Now the man thinks that maybe it's going to be too tall an order, and he settles down for a decent evening's drinking. After a couple of hours the beer brain takes over and he starts to think, "You know, I reckon I could chin that 'Kila, take out that 'croc and I could do that bird – hell, yes!" So he shouts for the owner to come out and watch him pass the test: "Gizza go on that tequila, why don'tcha?" The owner puts the gallon jar of tequila on the bar and the man picks it up. He drains the whole huge bottle without saying a word and the tears stream from his eyes. Then he walks outside and for the next 20 minutes the sound of beating, ripping and screaming come from the backyard. Then, the door is kicked open and the man is standing there with his shirt ripped to shreds, covered in mud and sweat and panting for breath. And he says, "Now, where the hell's that woman with the bad tooth?"

****

There's a regular-drinking guy whose local is called Sally's Legs after an old song. One Friday he knocks off work early, planning to spend the entire evening there getting steadily drunk. Unfortunately he doesn't count on the bar not opening until after work time, so he is forced to sit and wait for the staff to show up. As he is parked outside, a suspicious policeman walks up to his window and raps on it. "Yes, officer?" he says, "what can I do for you?" "What do you think you're doing hanging around here at this time of day?" says the policeman. "Well, sir," says the man, "I'm just waiting for Sally's Legs to open so I can be the first in to get a drink!"

****

A drunken bum has too much to drink one night in his local. He can hardly stand up, but he knows that he absolutely has to take a piss. He staggers over to the toilets, getting his cock out as he does so. He crashes through the door, penis in hand, only to bump into two women because he's stumbled into the ladies instead. One of the women screams and shouts, "This is for ladies, my good man!" and the bum replies, as he fumbles to put away his thing, "So is this, lady!"

****

Once upon a time there was a very keen policeman who liked to hang around outside bars and nab people as they left to drive home with too much alcohol inside them. One night he's waiting outside his regular haunt and he sees someone come staggering out. The guy walks up to first one car and tries his key in the lock, then the next and then the next. None of them open for him and it isn't until he gets to the fifth car in the car park that he gets in and, after five minutes' fumbling, starts the engine. He backs the car up, narrowly missing most of the others in the car park, and he wheelspins across the road and away. The keen policeman follows him quickly with his lights already flashing and his siren screaming. He pulls the guy over only just round the corner from the bar and takes it easy as he warns him and gives him the breathalyzer test. To the by-now-smug cop's surprise, the guy does not seem to have a drop of alcohol in his system. "What's that all about then?" asks the amazed young policeman, to which the man replies, "I'm tonight's designated decoy, officer!"

****

A man is sitting in a rough bar drinking. He orders a fresh pint, but is suddenly overcome with the urge to go to the toilet. He doesn't trust anyone in the crummy bar, but he has to go, so he scribbles on a cigarette paper, "I spat in this: don't drink it!" and he gums the paper to the side of his pint glass. He goes off to the toilet and comes back a couple of minutes later to find another cigarette paper stuck to his glass. On it is written, "So did we!"

****

A little boy and his younger brother were bored one day so decided to do interesting, grown-up stuff like swearing. The older boy says to his brother, "I know: next time we're downstairs with mum, I'll say 'Hell' and you can say 'Ass' – how's about that?" The younger boy nods his agreement and they troop off downstairs to have their breakfast. As they walk into the kitchen their mother says to the older child, "And what would you like for your breakfast, dear?" to which he replies, "Well, hell, mum, I'd like some cornflakes please." Upon hearing such profanity, the mother whacks the child really hard around the back of the head. The boy starts crying and runs off upstairs. The mother turns to the younger boy and looks him square in the face. "And what would you like for your breakfast, young man?" she says. "I don't really know, mum," he starts to say, "but you can bet your ass it won't be cornflakes!"

****

A farmer is in court fighting for a large insurance claim following a serious road accident he didn't cause. He is being questioned by the insurance company's lawyer and is being given a hard time because of his conflicting statements. The lawyer asks, "So, Farmer Brown; you are trying to claim substantial damages from the person you claim caused the accident, yet I have a sworn statement from the police officer who was present at the scene claiming that when asked how you were feeling immediately following the accident you said, and I quote, 'I'm fine, officer; in fact I've never felt better in my life!'" There is a gasp around the courtroom. "Now, is this or is this not true, Farmer Brown?" continues the brief. "Well, yes, but…" the farmer starts, but he is interrupted by the barrister: "Just a simple yes or no answer will suffice, Farmer Brown." "Yes," says Farmer Brown. After a while, it was the turn of the lawyer for the farmer's insurance to question him. "So, Farmer Brown, tell us the exact circumstances surrounding your statement of good health that my learned friend just made you discuss," the barrister says to the farmer. "Well, sir, as I was trying to say," Farmer Brown explains, "I had just had this horrific accident and I was lying in the middle of the road injured. My horse had been injured, too, and so had my dog. So, after a little while a policeman comes up to the horse, sees it struggling for life and shoots it. Then he walks over to my dog, hears it howling and shoots it. Then he walks over to me, bleeding on the ground, and says, 'How are you, sir?' Now what the hell would you have said in those circumstances?"

****

It's a beautiful day in County Kerry and people all over the county are sitting outside the pubs enjoying stout by the pint. In a cosy pub one man turns to his friend and says, "You see that man over there?" His friend nods. "Have you noticed that he's the spitting image of me? It's bloody uncanny, that's what it is, to be sure. I'm going to go over there and ask him a few questions: after all, 'tis not every day that you get to meet someone who could be your exact double, now is it?" And off he goes to see the man he is talking about. He taps him on the shoulder and says, "Excuse me, I couldn't help noticing from over there that you look almost exactly the same as me. I was thinking what an incredible coincidence that was!" "Me too, me too," replies the man, "I noticed you earlier and I was just about to come over and talk when I saw you coming over anyway. 'Tis an incredible thing to be sure. So whereabouts are you from?" he asks. "Well, I'm from Galway, originally," says the first man. "No, that's incredible!" says the second, "Me too! It's just unbelievable. What street did you live in?" "Why, I lived in Moher Street for 20 years, so I did," comes the reply from the first man. "No! I can't believe it – I did, too," says the second. "And what number in that street was it?" he asks. "Why, I lived in number 20." "Unbelievable," comes the reply, "that's the number I lived in. And what were your parents' names?" "Ruari and Siobhan," comes the reply. "This really is uncanny," the first man says, "those are the exact names of my parents, too!" At this point the two men continue talking and the new bar staff turn up for their shift. The new guy asks, "Anything happening?" and the guy about to go replies, "No, not really; just the Rix twins drunk again!"

****

A man walks into a bar. It is totally empty apart from the barman, who walks over to serve him. The man buys his beer and sits down in a corner. He then decides he'd like a chaser, so he walks up to the bar again. The barman has just gone out back for a second, but the guy hears a little squeaky voice say, "Nice shirt, mate." He looks around and he can't see anyone anywhere. He turns around to go and sit down and hears a similar voice say, "Great arse." He spins around quickly but he can't see anyone and the barman is definitely still out back. The man is a bit put out so he decides to go and buy some smokes. As he approaches the cigarette machine he hears the most dreadful swearing, aimed at him. "You miserable wanker piece of crap; you suck, you dumbarse twat!" The insults seem to be pouring from the machine, so he retreats and goes back to the bar. The barman is back by this time, so the man asks him, "Look, pal; what's going on with the funny voices in this place?" The barman looks at him and says, "Of course, well, you must mean the complimentary peanuts; and I'm sorry, but the cigarette machine is out of order!"

****

A trampy-looking man walks into a bar with a small dog under his arm. He walks straight up to the bar and puts the dog on it. The barman tells him that animals aren't allowed in the bar and that he'll have to leave. The man says that this dog is special, that it can talk and that if anyone wants to bet him $500 he'll take them on. The bartender laughs, but decides to indulge the old guy anyway and takes him up on the bet. So the guy turns to the dog and says slowly, "Now, Jock; what do we call the thing on top of this bar that keeps the rain off our heads when the weather's bad and the sun off our heads when the weather's good?" The dog shakes his head and then barks, "ROOF!" The barman looks at the man and bursts out laughing. "I'm not paying for that crap – you must be joking!" So the man says, "OK, OK, I'll show you again," and he turns to the dog and says slowly, "Jock, who was the greatest baseball player of all time?" The dog shakes his head and then barks, "RUTH!" The bartender hops over the bar, picks up the dog and the man and throws them both out. As they both lie on the sidewalk the dog looks up at the man and says sheepishly, "Should I have answered DiMaggio?"

✱✱✱✱

Had it off yet?

2

Jokes for the
healing process

A man is suffering from premature ejaculation, so he decides to see a doctor about it. The doctor says there is nothing physically wrong with the man, but that he has a mental block. The doctor suggests that to cure the problem the man should try to shock himself when he feels that he is about to ejaculate. The doctor suggests using a starting pistol: the man should fire it when he feels the need, and that this should help prevent the problem. The man thanks the doctor and runs off to the sports shop to get himself a starting pistol. He rushes home to his wife, whom he finds naked on the bed, all ready for him. Things go well, and they find themselves in the 69 position. Moments later, the man feels the urge to ejaculate, so pulls the trigger.

The next day the man finds himself back at the doctor's surgery. The doctor asks, "So, how did it go? Any improvements?" "Not really," begins the man, "when I fired the pistol, my wife crapped on my face and bit three inches off my penis, and my neighbour jumped naked out of the cupboard with his hands in the air!"

✳✳✳✳

At a conference, four surgeons are discussing operating on people from different professions. The first surgeon says, "My favourite are accountants. I love to open up accountants: when you do, everything is numbered." The second surgeon says, "Not bad, but you should try electricians. I love to open up electricians: when you do, everything is colour-coded." The third surgeon says, "Not bad, but you should try filing clerks. I love to open up filing clerks: when you do, everything is in alphabetical order." The fourth surgeon says, "Not bad, not bad, but you're all wrong. The easiest to operate on are lawyers. I love to open up lawyers: when you do, there are no guts, no heart, no spine, and the head and arse are completely interchangeable!"

****

A man goes to his doctor complaining that he cannot get his wife pregnant. The doctor is a little surprised because the man is 75. Not wishing to stand in his way, however, the doctor asks the man to provide him with a sperm sample and gives him a jar to place it in. Two days later the old man walks back into the surgery and gives the doctor the empty jar back. "What's that all about?" asks the doctor and the man begins his explanation. "Well, first of all, doc I tried with my left hand. That didn't work, so I tried with my right hand. That didn't work either, so I asked my wife to help. She's younger than me and she tried first with her left hand and then her right, but there was still no joy. Then she tried with her mouth – even between her teeth – but still nothing. As a last resort we called the neighbour over from next door. The woman tried, with both hands and then with the mouth, too, but it just really wouldn't work." The doctor was a bit shocked by this and asked, "Even your neighbour?" 'Yes, doc," said the man. "We tried and tried and tried, but no matter what we did, none of us could get the lid off that bloody jar!"

****

A really beautiful woman makes the mistake one day of going to see an unscrupulous gynaecologist. He is badly behaved at the best of times, but when he sets eyes on this fantastic-looking creature he can hardly hold himself back. He tells her to undress immediately and proceeds to examine her without even asking what her problem is. He begins by stroking her thigh. As he does so, he says, "Do you know what I'm doing?" and the woman replies, "Yes, doctor; you are checking the area around my pubic region for any abrasions or abnormalities in case my problems stem from there." "That's very good," says the doctor, who then begins to stroke her breasts. "And do you know what I'm doing now?" he asks. "Yes, doctor; you are checking me for any odd lumps or abnormalities in my mammary region." "That's very good," says the doctor, who then takes out his "pork thermometer" and proceeds to rub it on the woman's pussy. "And do you know what I'm doing now?" he asks. "Yes, doctor," the woman replies. "You are contracting herpes, which is the reason I came in here today!"

****

A man and a woman meet up at a party. They get on well and it is lust at first sight, so they go back to the woman's house to make the beast with two backs. They are getting it on and the man takes off his shirt and then the woman's shirt. He then gets up and washes his hands. A few minutes later he removes his trousers and her skirt. He then gets up and washes his hands. A few minutes later he removes his underwear and then her underwear. He then gets up and washes his hands. After this the woman gives him a strange look and says, "You must be a dentist." "Why, that's right," he says. "How on earth did you know?" "Easy," she says. "You wash your hands after every procedure, and the only people who do that are dentists." So they carry on, and they end up having sex. Afterwards, when the dentist has washed his hands, they are talking. The woman says, "You must be a really good dentist." The man replies, "Why, yes; I am, as it happens. I was top in my class at dental academy and I have won prizes around the world for my dentistry. How do you know?" The woman says, "Because I didn't feel a thing!"

****

A husband and wife are talking one night at dinner and the wife announces that she's thinking of having her breasts enlarged with plastic surgery. The husband says, "You don't need to pay some quack to make your tits bigger, honey: I know how you can do it for pretty much nothing!" "Oh, really?" says the wife, "and how would that be then?" "Just rub toilet paper in between your tits twice a day," says the husband. "Oh, really?" says the wife, "and how on earth does that work, then?" "I don't know," says the husband, "but it sure did the trick for your arse!"

****

A man goes to hospital for a circumcision operation and he wakes up in the morning surrounded by hospital staff. He wonders what the hell is going on and then he feels an enormous piece of padding between his legs. The head surgeon says to him, "Look here, sir; we're all really, really sorry, but I'm afraid we made a mistake and got a bit carried away with the chopping. We've ended up giving you a complete sex change operation." The man screams and shouts and cries his eyes out. "Oh, my God," he says eventually. "There's so much I'll never be able to do again. I will never, ever be able to experience an erection." The head surgeon strokes him on the head and says, "Of course you will, of course you will. It just won't be yours, that's all!"

****

A man and a woman could not have children and spent a long time working out why this was. Eventually it turned out that it was the man's problem, so they decided to get the woman artificially inseminated. They booked an appointment at the clinic, but at the last minute the husband was called away on urgent business, so the wife had to go alone. She walked into the clinic and was shown to her room for insemination. After a couple of minutes a doctor walked in and told her to remove her clothes from the bottom half of her body and to lie back on the bed with her feet in the stirrups. The woman complied. After she had done this, the doctor dropped his trousers and pants and began to walk towards her. "Er, doctor, what on earth are you doing?" she asked, a little worried. "What's the problem?" said the doctor. "Don't you want to get pregnant?" "Well, yes, doctor, I do…" began the wife. "Well, just lie back and think of England," said the doctor, "because we're out of the bottled variety and you'll have to take what's on tap!"

****

A man goes to the doctor with a strange problem. "Doctor, whenever I break wind there is no smell at all. It's really strange and no matter what I eat, I get the same result – no smell whatsoever!" The doctor has a cursory investigation and then asks the man if he can possibly break wind there and then. The man drops his trousers and pants and farts extremely loudly. The doctor sniffs at the air a couple of times and immediately says, "Oh yes, this is a common one. I know exactly what the problem is," and he walks out of the room. He comes straight back with a six-foot pole with a large brass hook on the end. "Jesus Christ, doctor; what the hell are you going to do with that pole?" asks the man. "I'm going to open the bloody window," says the doctor, "You've got a blocked nose!"

****

"Doctor, I'm not feeling so well," says the patient. "Would it be possible to run some tests?" "Sure thing," says the doctor. "Stop by the surgery some time today and ask the nurse. Bring a urine sample, too. We'll talk about the results over the phone." The patient does as instructed and waits for the results. One day passes: nothing. The following day he gets a phone call from his doctor who says: "Well, I have good news and bad news." "What is the good news?" the patient asks. "You have 24 hours left to live." "WHAT??? What's the bad news, then ??" "I forgot to call you yesterday."

****

A psychiatrist and a proctologist became good friends and agreed to share offices to cut down on expenses. To economize even further, they had just one sign printed:

Dr John Wayland, Psychiatrist

Dr Stan Smith, Proctologist

SPECIALIZING IN ODDS AND ENDS

****

A man has been suffering from a tenacious cold for the past week. He goes to his doctor, who prescribes him some tablets. A week later, the same guy comes back, every bit as ill as before. Frowning, the doctor prescribes him a stronger version of the drugs and sends him home. It doesn't work, though, and the man comes back a week later just as miserable as before. The medicine obviously doesn't work and the doctor reckons it is a case of "intractable cold of an unknown nature". "All right," says the doctor. "What I want you to do is to open your bedroom window tonight and spend an hour naked in front of it." "What?" exclaims the patient. "I'll catch pneumonia!" "Pneumonia is fine," the doctor replies. "I can treat pneumonia."

****

A nurse walks into a ward to see patients early in the morning. "Well, nurse, it seems to me you got up from the wrong side of the bed this morning," says one patient. "Why do you say that?" "You're wearing the surgeon's slippers."

****

After years of battling with himself, John finally went to a psychiatrist. "Doc," he said, "I've got trouble. Every time I get into bed, I think there's somebody under it. If I get under the bed, I think there's somebody on top of it. I *know* there's no one in my bed or under my bed, but it doesn't matter, I have to check. You have to help me, it's been going on for years and I am going mad." "It's all in your head. Just put yourself in my hands for two years," said the shrink. "Come to me three times a week, and I'll cure your fears." "How much do you charge?" asked John, suspiciously. "€50 per visit." "€50, three times a week, for two years?" chokes John. "No way!" and he storms off. Six months later the doctor meets John on the street. "Why didn't you ever come to see me again?" asked the psychiatrist. "€50 a visit? A bartender cured me for the price of a beer." "Is that so?" says the doctor scornfully, "how?" "He told me to cut the legs off the bed!"

★★★★

A lady wanted bigger breasts, so she went to her doctor to refer her to a plastic surgeon. "I can do that," said her doctor, "but I would like you to try a simple exercise before surgery or drugs." He stood up to demonstrate, holding his arms straight out to the side, rotating them counter-clockwise, and singing, "Ashes to ashes, dust to dust, if I do this enough, I'll have a big bust." "Do that as often as you can and come back in a week." One week later, she's back at the doctor, and tells him that it didn't work. "How often have you done the exercise?" the doctor asks her. "Three to four times a day," she says. "Bah! Not nearly half enough!" the doctor scoffs. "Do it at least 30 to 40 times a day and come back in a week." She tries this, performing the exercise whenever she can, which means that she does it on her local Tesco parking lot, before getting into her car. "Ashes to ashes, dust to dust, if I do this enough, I'll have a big bust." The driver of the car parked next to hers turns around, looks at her with round eyes and asks: "Do you see Dr. Johnson?" "Well, yes, as a matter of fact. How did you know?" she queries. The man faces her, places both hands on his hips, moves his hips in a circular motion, and says, "Hickory dickory dock…"

****

A young lady entered the doctor's office carrying an infant. "Doctor," she explained, "the baby seems to be ailing. Instead of gaining weight, he lost three ounces this week." The doctor examined the child and then started to squeeze the lady's breasts. Too stunned to react, she lets him unbutton her blouse, deftly removing the bra and stroking her right nipple, emitting a thoughtful "Mmmm…" "Young lady," he announced, "No wonder the baby is losing weight, you haven't got any milk!" "Of course not!" she shrieked. "It's not my child, it's my sister's!"

****

After the baby was born, the panicked Japanese father went to see the obstetrician. "Doctor," he said, "I'm a little upset. You see, my baby daughter has red hair. She can't possibly be mine." "Do not worry," the doctor said genially. "Even though you and your wife both have black hair, one of your ancestors might have contributed red hair to the gene pool." "This is impossible," the man insisted. "We're pure Oriental. There have never been redheads in any of our families." "Well," said the doctor, "let me ask you this. How often do you have sex?" The man seemed ashamed. "I've been working very hard for the past year. We only made love once or twice a month." "There you have it!" the doctor said confidently. "It's just rust."

****

Three patients in a mental institution prepare for an examination given by the head psychiatrist. If the patients pass the exam, they will be free to leave the hospital and go back to a normal life. However, if they fail, the institution will detain them for another five years. The doctor takes the three patients to the top of a diving board looking over an empty swimming pool, and asks the first patient to jump. The first patient jumps headfirst into the pool and breaks both arms. The second patient, who has just witnessed what has happened, jumps enthusiastically into the empty pool and breaks both legs. The third patient looks over the side and backs off from the diving board. "Congratulations! You're a free man. Just tell me: why didn't you jump?" asked the doctor. "Well, doc, I can't swim!"

****

A man, looking like a mechanic in stained overalls, comes into the reception of the posh local surgery, full of mothers and their children, well-to-do professionals and retired people looking at him with disdain.

He approaches the receptionist and says, in a voice that is altogether too loud for this sort of place: "There's something wrong with my dick." "We don't use this kind of language here," says the nurse reprovingly. "Please try again and be more polite this time: say you have a problem with your ear or something." The man seems about to explode but, with visible effort, decides just to let it go. He takes a deep breath and says: "There is a problem with my ear." "Is there, my dear?" the receptionist says smugly. "What kind of problem?" The man gives her an evil grin and says: "I can't piss out of it."

✳✳✳✳

Bill has a problem and goes to the doctor. He has trouble getting an erection. The doctor examines him fully and explains to him that he's got a problem with the muscles around the base of his penis. They are very damaged and there is currently no known treatment. The doctor does offer a solution, however, and that is a new experimental cure which involves grafting muscles from a baby elephant's trunk onto the base of his penis. Bill is a bit worried by this, but he figures it's better to try and fail rather than never to have sex again, so he agrees to try it out. Months later, Bill is fully recovered from the operation and finds that everything is functioning normally. He takes his girlfriend out for a candlelit dinner with the hope of a romantic encounter later. About halfway through the meal, Bill starts to feel uncomfortable around his groin and the feeling gets worse and worse as the meal continues. Eventually Bill can bear it no longer and unzips his fly to release the pressure. As soon as he does this, his penis springs out, bounces to the top of the table, grabs a bread roll and returns to his underpants. His girlfriend squeals with shock – and possibly delight. "Bill – that was amazing! Can you do it again?" Bill replies, "Probably, darling, but I don't think I've got room up my arse for another bread roll!"

****

It took Bob a little while to accept the fact that his penis seemed to grow. Of course he was delighted, as was his wife, but it soon grew to an impressive 20 inches and Bob decided it was time to go and see a doctor. After an initial examination, the physician explained to the couple that, though rare, Bob's condition could be cured through corrective surgery. "We just have to operate – a simple thing, really – and all will be fine again." "And how long will Bob be on crutches?" the wife asked anxiously. "Crutches? Why would he need crutches?" the surprised doctor asked. "Well," said the wife suspiciously, "You are planning to lengthen Bob's legs, aren't you?"

****

The doctor entered the waiting room. "I have some good news for you, Mrs Douglas." "Pardon me," she interrupted coldly, "but it's Miss." The doctor corrected himself and said, "I have some bad news for you, Miss Douglas."

****

A woman went to her doctor for a follow-up visit after the doctor had prescribed testosterone (a male hormone) to her. She was a little worried about some of the side effects she was experiencing. "Doctor, the hormones you've been giving me have really helped. I feel much better, but I'm wondering if you got the dosage right. I've started growing hair in places that I've never grown hair before." The doctor reassured her. "A little hair growth is a perfectly normal side effect of testosterone. Just where has this hair appeared?" "On my balls."

****

A woman went to the surgery. She was seen by one of the new doctors, but after about four minutes in the examination room she burst out, screaming as she ran down the hall. An older doctor stopped and asked her what the problem was, and she explained, obviously in shock. The older doctor marched back to the first and demanded, "What's the matter with you? Mrs Johnston is 67 years old: she has four grown children and seven grandchildren, and you told her she was pregnant?" The new doctor smiled smugly as he continued to write on his clipboard. "Cured her hiccups though, didn't I?"

****

A man goes to the doctor with a terrible problem with bad breath. "I've tried everything, doctor," he says, nearly in tears. "I changed toothpaste ten times, tried mints, mouthwash, you name it. I can't get rid of this terrible odour." The doctor nods and asks the guy to get undressed. After a thorough examination, he allows him to put his clothes back on. "You seem to have a rash around your anus. We will have to treat this first. In the meantime, try not to chew your fingernails."

****

A man walks into the office of an eminent psychiatrist and sits down to explain his problem. "Yes, well, you see, I've got this problem," the man says. "I keep hallucinating that I'm a dog. A large, white, hairy Dulux dog. It's crazy. I don't know what to do!" "Ah, a common canine complex," said the doctor soothingly. "It's all right: we can cure this together if we work hard and concentrate. Come over here, lie down on the couch and tell me more about it." "Oh no, doctor. I'm not allowed on the furniture," the man says, horrified.

****

A few days before his proctological exam, a one-eyed man accidentally swallowed his glass eye. He was worried for a while and kind of expected to see it pop up at some point, but there were no ill effects, it didn't re-appear, and so he forgot about it. The day for the appointment arrived and he was lying on his belly, after having changed into a surgical gown behind a screen. The doctor approached, lifted the gown up and came face to face with the glass eye stuck in his patient's anus staring right back at him. "You know," he says in a gentle, reproving tone, "you should learn to trust me better than that."

****

A busy doctor in an ER department is rushing down the corridor when he is stopped by a nurse who needs him to sign a patient's chart. The doctor reaches behind his ear puts the pen in his mouth in concentration while reading the form, before spitting out in horror. "Arghhh," he cries, realizing he's been sucking on the wrong end of a thermometer. "some arsehole's got my pen again!"

****

A young woman was going to marry one of those elderly, wealthy eccentrics who want a virgin bride. Since she wasn't, she went to a doctor to reconstruct her hymen. The doctor told her that would cost around €500 to do it surgically, but that there was another way that would cost only €50 and could be done straight away in his office. The woman agreed to try the cheap way, paid the money and lay down on the consultation bed, feet in the stirrups. The doctor worked on her for several minutes, then congratulated her on her forthcoming marriage and showed her the door. After the honeymoon, the woman came back to the doctor and told him that it was perfect: the pain, the blood, everything was there. "How did you do it?" she asked. "Very simple," he replied. "I tied your pubic hair together."

****

A man comes to a doctor and, twitching his fingers and stuttering, finally manages to say, "Doctor, I have a... er... sexual performance problem. Can you help me?" "Oh, that's not a problem for us men anymore!" announces the proud physician with a broad wink. "This new pill just came out – a new wonder drug called Miagra. That does the trick! You take a few of these and it's the end of your problems!" So the doctor gives the man a prescription for a packet of Miagra and sends him on his merry way. A couple of months later, the doctor runs into his patient on the street. "Doctor, doctor!" exclaims the man excitedly, "I've got to thank you! This drug is a miracle! It's wonderful!" "Well, I'm glad to hear that," says the physician, rather pleased with himself. "And what does your wife think about it?" "Wife?" the guy said with a silly grin on his face, "I haven't been home yet!"

****

An attractive young woman goes for her annual check-up and is asked by the new doctor to get undressed, for he must take her temperature rectally to be sure. She agrees, but a few minutes later says indignantly, "Doctor, that's not my rectum!" "Madam," says the doctor, "that's not my thermometer."

****

The only treatment to save a patient is a brain transplant. His family is gathered in the doctor's office, taking in the bad news. "Er, doctor, how much is this going to cost?" "Well, it's about £600,000 for a male brain and £200,000 for a female brain," the specialist answers. The men in the room all sit up and start chuckling, a superior expression appearing on their faces. The youngest daughter casts her eyes towards the ceiling and asks the doctor: "And why is a female brain cheaper?" "Oh, it's standard practice, Miss," he replies. "The brain has to be marked down because it's used."

****

A guy walks into the doctor's office and says, "D-d-d-doct-tor-r-r, I've b-been st-t-tuttering f-for y-y-years and I-I-I-I'm t-t-tired of it. C-c-can y-y-you he-he-help me?" The doctor examines him swiftly and says, "Well I think I know what the problem is." The guy says, "W-w-well, w-w-what is it, d-doc?" The doctor says, "Well, it's your penis you see: it's about a foot long and all the downward pressure is putting a strain on your vocal cords." The guy says, "I d-d-d-didn't kn-n-n-n-now it c-c-c-could c-c-cause a p-p-p-p... p-p-p-p-p... p-p-problem. W-w-what c-c-can we d-do?" The doctor advises, "Well, I can cut it off and transplant a shorter one. The pressure will disappear and so will your stutter" The guy thinks for a minute then says, "D-d-do it!" He has the operation and, three weeks later, he returns to see the doctor and says, "Doc, you solved the problem and I don't stutter anymore, but I've only had sex once in the past three weeks. My wife doesn't like it anymore. She liked it with my long one. I don't care if I have to stutter: I want you to put my long one back on." The doctor says, "N-n-n-no. A d-d-d-deal's a d-d-d-deal!!!"

****

A rather embarrassed man goes to see his doctor and tells him: "Well, I have this problem, you see: I can't get it up for my wife anymore, if you see what I mean." "It's quite all right," the doctor says. "Get undressed and we'll see what the problem is." He does so, but can find nothing wrong with the patient. "Come back tomorrow," he advises. "Bring your wife with you. I'd like to examine her, too." The anxious patient turns up the following day with his wife, as promised. The doctor has a quick look at the woman, then asks her to take her clothes off. "Mmm… I see… Now turn around please. Mmmm… Can you crouch down for me? That's it. Gooooood, now get on all fours on the carpet. Yes, this way… Mmmm… It's OK, you can put your clothes back on." While the wife is getting dressed, the doctor takes the husband aside and tells him: "You're perfectly healthy. Don't worry. Your wife didn't give me an erection either."

****

After a long time procrastinating, a man finally agrees to see a doctor about a lump on his belly, but only if his grown-up son goes with him. On the appointed day, they receive the terrible news that he is suffering from cancer and that he doesn't have long to live. They are both shocked and the son decides to take his dad to his local for a pick-me-up. In the pub they find all his father's friends and his dad tells them in hushed tones that he is going to die of AIDS. The son is rather surprised and, when they find a table to sit at for a chat, he asks his dad: "Tell me; why did you tell your friends you're dying of AIDS? You don't have AIDS." "I know," the father replies, "but I don't want them screwing your mother after I'm gone!"

****

It is the ophthalmologist's 40th birthday and, in the middle of the party, he is blindfolded and taken by the hand to a table in the centre of the dining room. His loving wife takes the blindfold off with a flourish and he finds himself in front of a huge cake with 40 eyes made of marzipan around it. The specialist stares at the cake and then erupts in laughter. He laughs so much that a couple of his friends have to pick him up from the floor. After a few minutes, wiping a tear of mirth from his eye, he says: "I'm sorry: this is a great cake. It's just that I suddenly thought about my colleague Terry, who's a gynaecologist. It's his 50th birthday tomorrow."

✳✳✳✳

A new clinic, with several different specialists, opened in a trendy part of the city. Wanting to be different and creative with the design, the administration decided that each doctor's office door would, in some way, be representative of his practice. So, when construction was complete… the eye doctor's door had a peep-hole, the orthopaedist's door had a broken hinge, the psychiatrist's door was painted all kinds of crazy colours. As for the gynaecologist's door, it was left open… just a crack.

✳✳✳✳

A man staggers into hospital with two black eyes and a golf club tightly wrapped round his throat. The doctor on duty asks him what happened. "Well, doc, it was like this," the man says. "I was out for a quiet round of golf with the missus and she shanked her ball something terrible. It landed in a field full of cows, so we both went to look for it. I was having a good look round but couldn't find it. Anyway, I noticed a white thing in the arse of one of the cows so I walked over, lifted up its tail and there was my wife's golf ball, rammed right up there. That's when I made my only mistake." "And what was that, then?" asked the doc. "Well, I turned to get my wife's attention, lifted the cow's tail and shouted, 'Hey! This looks like yours!'"

****

A doctor is having an affair with his young, enthusiastic, if a bit dumb, nurse. The nurse gets pregnant and the doctor, of course, doesn't want his wife to know. So he says to his mistress: "You go and lie low somewhere, say Italy, for a while, until the baby is due. When the baby is born, just send me a postcard with 'Spaghetti' written on it and I'll know. By this time, I'll have spoken to my wife." "Why spaghetti?" she asks. "Because you'll be in Italy, that's why," the doctor says, just on this side of panicking. Not finding anything logical to reply to that, the girl agrees and flies off to Italy. After nine months, the doctor receives a call from his wife, who tells him she has just received the strangest postcard. "Don't worry, honey," the doctor says. "I'm coming home and I'll explain everything." Back home, he picks up the postcard, wondering what he is going to say to his wife, reads it, stares at it for a second or two and then topples over and dies of a massive heart attack. Stunned, her wife re-reads the mysterious postcard through tears of grief. It says: "Spaghetti, spaghetti, spaghetti, spaghetti, three with sausage and meatballs, one with mussels."

****

A famous heart surgeon is having a friendly charity barbecue when he is approached by a loudmouth. "Hey, Doc," the guy says, "I'm the best mechanic in town. I can take an engine apart, take the valves out, clean them, tune them and after I put everything back together the baby will purr like a newborn kitten. We're basically doing the same job, so how come you get more money than me, hey?" "Try to do that with the engine running," the heart surgeon says softly.

****

A 92-year-old man went to the doctor to get a physical check-up. A few days later, the doctor saw the man walking down the street with a gorgeous young lady on his arm. A couple of days later, when the old man had an appointment with the doctor again, the doctor said, "You're really doing great, aren't you? You seem chirpy enough!" The man replied, "Just doing what you said, doctor: 'Get a hot mama and be cheerful,' and it works wonders." Horrified, the doctor said: "I didn't say that! I said, 'You've got a heart murmur. Be careful!'"

****

A man goes to see a doctor and tells him he hasn't been feeling very well lately. The doctor examines him for a few minutes and then takes three jars of big coloured pills from a medicine cabinet. "Here is your treatment: you are going to take this green pill in the morning, with a big glass of water, then the yellow pill after lunch, with a big glass of water and finally this red pill, again with a big glass of water. As you can see, these pills are pretty big, you might actually need two glasses of water at night." The patient stares at the huge pills, horrified. "Jeez, doc; that's a lot of pills... Er... what exactly is my problem?" "You're not drinking enough water," the doctor replied.

****

A young man enters the doctor's office complaining of being run-down. "Well, what can I say?" says the doctor. "Book a few days off and rest – take a vacation, even: spend the weekend at home and sleep." "I can't do that, doctor," the young man replies, shaking his head. "I work in the stock market; it's a very profitable line of work and I'll lose a lot of money if I take time off." "In that case, change your lifestyle, don't go clubbing and so on: cut down on sex, for instance." "What? I'm a young man, I'm in my prime, and you want me to give up sex?" "Well, you could get married," the doctor mused. "That way you could taper off gradually."

****

One afternoon, two new doctors from India were having an animated discussion in a corridor of an American hospital. "I say it's spelled 'W-H-O-O-M'," said the first Indian doctor. "No, you're mistaken: it is spelled 'W-H-O-M-B'," said the other Indian doctor. A haughty American nurse passing by said smugly, "Excuse me: you are both wrong. It is spelled 'W-O-M-B'." "Thank you, nurse," said one of the doctors, rather coldly, "but we prefer to settle this argument ourselves.

Besides, I don't think you're in a position to describe the sound of an elephant passing wind under water, are you?"

✳✳✳✳

Two friends were deaf-mutes and had grown up together, attending the same schools and everything. After university they had lost touch but one day, ten years later, they met up again in the street, quite by chance. They got around to talking via sign language and they chatted for ages. It turned out that one of them was no longer mute but had learned to talk. The other guy was amazed and was also really curious to know exactly how his friend had learned to talk after all this time. The guy who could now talk explained to his friend that he'd visited an extraordinary doctor who had performed revolutionary new surgery on him, but that it was rather expensive. He gave his friend the doctor's address and bade him good day. The deaf-mute hopped straight into a cab and shot over to the address. He was given an interview with the doctor straight away, and the doctor explained that he would have to come in every day for 26 days and that the course would cost him exactly one million euro. The man thought this very expensive but agreed, having seen the result on his friend earlier that day. He paid the money and begged the doctor to start on him right away. The doctor agreed and asked the man to strip naked and to lie on the examination table. The doctor walked over to the cupboard in the room and took out a broom handle with a doorknob on the end and a huge jar of Vaseline. The doctor dipped the doorknob in Vaseline and, taking a running leap, proceeded to shove the whole lot up the deaf-mute's arse. "Aaaaaaaaaaaaaaah!"

screamed the deaf-mute. "Very good," replied the doctor, "and tomorrow we'll work on 'B'."

****

A dentist is treating a Buddhist monk for a nasty cavity and is quite surprised to hear the patient say no to painkillers. "But why?" the dentist asks. "It is just an anaesthetic." "I want to transcend dental medication," the monk replies.

****

"My husband and I have been trying anal sex recently," the woman says, somewhat red-cheeked, to her doctor. "I mean, is this OK?" "Do you enjoy it?" the doctor asks. "As a matter of fact, we do," she replies "Does it hurt you?" "No, it's fine," she replies. "Well, I don't see why you shouldn't carry on, as long as you're careful not to get pregnant." "Pregnant?" the woman says, astonished. "I can get pregnant this way?" "Well, of course: where do you think lawyers come from?" the doctor replies.

****

A woman had just given birth to her first baby. She was tired and haggard, but she noticed that the baby was nowhere to be seen. "Where's my baby?" she asks. "I want to see my baby." The doctor, apologizing, says: "Er, well, you see, mmm... I know it will come as a shock, but there's a problem with your baby: she has no arms..."

The mother is stunned. "Wh... What..? No arms?" Then she wails: "I don't care: she's my baby – I want to see my baby! I hurt all this time to get her: I want to see her!" "Er..." says the doctor, eyes downcast, "you see, she has no legs either..." The mother is speechless for a few seconds, then erupts in tears and wails: "I want to see my baby!" The doctor relents and nods to the nurse outside, who brings in a cot. The blonde mother peers inside and the smile dies on her face. Inside the cot is a big ear. "Is... is this my baby?" she whispers. "Speak louder," says the doctor, "she's deaf."

****

A woman has twins and, because she can't take care of them properly, gives them up for adoption. One of them goes to a family in Egypt and is named Ahmal. The other goes to a family in Spain; they name him Juan. Years later, Juan sends a picture of himself to his birth mother. Upon receiving the picture, she goes to see her doctor and says: "I feel so bad! I want to see my children again! Look, Juan sent me a picture!" She hands the picture over to the doctor. "I want a picture of his brother, too!" she wails. Her doctor answers: "Come on, they're twins! If you've seen Juan, you've seen Ahmal."

****

Deep into an international flight, a guy finds himself desperate to go to the toilet. It is busy for ten, then 20, then 30 minutes. He calls the stewardess and asks if he cannot just use the ladies' toilet, just this once. She says that that will be fine, but that he mustn't use any of the buttons that he'll see on the wall. The man says that's fine and he promises not to press any of the buttons. So he goes to the bathroom and does his business, but all the time he's looking at these four buttons on the wall next to the toilet. He gets really curious and says to himself that nothing could be that bad, and that he'll just try the first button. So, he presses it. There is a noise, and suddenly a warm, gentle, soothing jet of warm water sprays from the toilet, cleaning his arse. "This is fantastic," thinks the man. "I must try the second button." So he presses the second button. There is a noise and warm air comes flowing up from the toilet, drying his arse. "This really is fantastic," he thinks to himself, "I've got to try the third button." So, he presses the third button. There is a noise and some gentle, soothing powder is deposited on his arse. "Unbelievable," he says to himself. "I really have to try the last button," which has the initials "ATR" stamped upon it. So he presses the fourth button and the next thing he knows he is waking up in a hospital bed, surrounded by doctors and covered in bandages. There is blood all over the place and he is hooked up to a drip. "What the hell happened to me?" he asks the nearest doctor. "You pressed the ATR button, didn't you?" says the doctor. "Well, yes," says the man, "but I never knew what it meant!" The doctor replies, "Automatic Tampon Removal!"

✳✳✳✳

A woman takes her 16-year-old daughter Chrissy to the doctor. "So, Mrs Jones, what's the problem?" he asks genially. The mother says, "Well, it's Chrissy. She keeps getting these cravings, she's putting on weight, and is sick most mornings." Sighing inwardly and guessing what he's going to find, the doctor nonetheless gives Chrissy an examination. Then he turns to the daughter and says, "Well, I don't know how to tell you this but, Chrissy, you're pregnant – about four months would be my guess." The mother says, "What? Pregnant?! She can't be: she's never, ever been left alone with a man! Have you, Chrissy?" Her daughter says, in tears, "No, mother! I've never even kissed a man!" The doctor slowly walks over to the window and just stares out for five minutes. Puzzled, the mother finally asks, "Is there something wrong out there doctor?" The doctor replies, as if coming out of a reverie, "No, not really: it's just that the last time something like this happened, a star appeared in the east and three wise men came over the hill. I'll be damned if I'm going to miss it this time!"

✱✱✱✱

A doctor and his wife are sitting in front of the TV one evening and the good doctor is relaxing by throwing peanuts in the air and catching them in his mouth and eating them. It goes on for a while until the end of the program, when a comment his wife makes distracts him and the peanut lands in his ear. He tries to shake it out, to no avail. Trying to take it out with his little finger, he just manages to get the damn thing even deeper. "Come on," says his worried wife. "Let's go to the hospital and get this out." The doctor agrees, sighs heavily and puts his coat on, just as their daughter comes back from the cinema with her boyfriend. He explains what has happened while his wife is looking for the car keys. On hearing the story the boyfriend comes forward and says he can help. He asks the good doctor to sit down again, unceremoniously sticks two fingers up his nose and tells him to blow as hard as he can. Sure enough, the peanut pops out of the doctor's ear and goes "Ping!" against the mirror on the mantelpiece. As the daughter and her boyfriend go through to the kitchen to get drinks, the doctor and his wife sit down to discuss their luck. "So," the wife says, "What do you think he'll become after he finishes school? A GP or a surgeon?" "Well," replies the doctor, rubbing his nose, "by the smell of his fingers, I think he's likely to be our son-in-law."

****

A friendly young doctor from a college town treated a lot of college-age girls. One day, one of them came in for a routine check-up. She took off her T-shirt to reveal a big, but faint, "H" shape on her chest. How curious, he thought, so asked her how she got it. "Oh that," she giggled. "That's Harvey, my boyfriend. He was so proud of getting into Harvard that he never takes his Harvard T-shirt off, even when we're in bed." The next day, another college girl came in for her check-up. She took off her T-shirt, and there was a big, but faint, "Y" shape on her chest. How curious, the doctor thought again, so asked her how she got it. "Oh that," she giggled, "that's Youssef, my boyfriend. He was so proud of getting into Yale that he never takes his Yale T-shirt off, even when we're in bed." The next day, a third college girl comes in for her check-up. She takes off her T-shirt, and there is a big but faint "M" on her chest. "Don't tell me – you have a boyfriend at Michigan," the doctor quips. "No, but I have a girlfriend at Wisconsin!" the girl replies.

****

The Smiths were having marital problems so they went to see an eminent sex therapist. After a couple of hours of tests he agreed to help them. The solution to their problem was for them to buy a pound of grapes and a dozen doughnuts on the way home. When they got back, they were to sit opposite each other, totally naked, and Mr Smith should roll the grapes across the floor and eat the ones that ended up in Mrs Smith, while she should throw the doughnuts at him, and eat the ones that stayed on him. A couple of weeks later, the Joneses came to see the same sex therapist. "Our friends the Smiths recommended you highly," they said. After a couple of hours of tests the therapist informed the Joneses that there was nothing he could do for them. "But you helped the Smiths, didn't you? What about us?" they said. After hours of begging, the therapist said that there was only one thing they could do and it wasn't guaranteed to work. "On your way back home, stop off and buy a pound of oranges and a packet of Polos…"

****

Fun things to do with an ambulance:

Drive too fast over speed bumps.

Stop with the siren on at a petrol station to fill it up.

Get involved in an accident.

Stop several times to ask for directions.

Drive by a McDonald's to ask if they want to buy fresh meat.

Shoot at the dogs which always chase the ambulance.

Replace the siren with the music of an ice-cream van.

If there's not enough work, drive over people yourself.

Fill the air tanks with liquids.

Ask your boss for the new Lamborghini Diablo ambulance.

Put a twirling disco light in the back.

Drive around the graveyard.

Paint "Satan loves you" on the side.

Throw bloody lamb chops out of the back door.

Keep circling the same block with your head out of the window and your tongue hanging out.

Drive to a morgue and ask if they've got any live ones they want you to take.

****

How many psychiatrists does it take to change a light bulb? Only one, but the light bulb has to want to change.

****

What does it mean when the doctor says you have six months to live? You have five months to pay.

****

In the Army Now

3

Jokes for the
regiment

The General arrived at his office on a Sunday morning and discovered that none of his private aides were there. Grimly, he remembered it had been one aide's birthday party the previous evening and he had no doubt as to what condition they were in. At around ten o'clock, five aides arrived, unshaved and dressed in rather piteous attire. They salute as smartly as they can and brace themselves for the General's grilling. "I presume you were at Smith's birthday party last night, weren't you?" "Sir, yes, Sir," one aide answers. "And you couldn't get up early enough this morning to get to the office because you were too drunk!" thundered the General. "Er, no, Sir," the aide said timidly, looking at his friends. "So what is your excuse, young man?" the General wondered, sitting down, with a dangerous, vicious smile on his lips. "I can explain. You see, we did run a little late, I admit. We ran to the bus but we missed it; we hailed a cab but it broke down; we found a farm and bought eight horses but they dropped dead; we ran ten miles, and now we're here. It's just a logistical problem, really, General, Sir!" The General eyed him suspiciously, but as he hadn't heard such a good one for a long time, he let the men go. An hour later, the last aide showed up, in the same dishevelled state. "Sorry, Sir," he said. "I ran late; tried to catch a bus but missed it; I hailed a cab but..." "Let me guess," the General interrupted. "The cab broke down, so you bought a horse in a farm but it died on you, so you ran for ten miles. Do you really think I'm going to swallow this?" "Er, no, Sir; you see, there were so many dead horses on the way that it took forever to go around them."

****

A famous Admiral and an equally famous General were fishing together in a boat when all of a sudden a squall came up. They both fell in the water and spent some time spluttering, struggling helplessly and swallowing quite a quantity of water, until the Admiral floundered his way back to the boat and pulled himself painfully in. Then he fished out the General. Catching his breath, he puffed: "Please don't say a word about this to anyone. If the Navy found out I can't swim, I'd be disgraced." "Don't worry," the General said ruefully. "Your secret is quite safe. I myself would hate to have my men find out I can't walk on water."

****

A guy comes to the military enlistment office. "What would you like to be?" the Officer asks him. "A pilot," he answers. "Good choice, son." The Officer enrols the guy and sends him to study flying. Unfortunately, he doesn't have what it takes to be a pilot and fails his exams. He is sent back to the military enlistment office again. "Sorry, but you can't be a pilot any more: I'm sure you can see that. Select something else." The guy thinks for a few seconds and speaks: "I want to be in the Air Defence." "First a pilot, then air defence? Why AD?" "If I can't fly, nobody will fly!" the guy answers pugnaciously.

****

A Corporal announces: "The platoon has been assigned to unload 'luminum…" "Er, aluminium, not 'luminum, Sir," corrects a trooper.

"The platoon is going to unload 'luminum," repeats the Corporal, "and the intellectual here is going to load shit."

****

The Captain calls for the Sergeant. "I have some bad news for Private Johnson," he tells him. "His mum died last night. I'd like you to break the news to him gently, you know: he's a good guy. Tell him to come and see me." The Sergeant nods, salutes and departs for the morning roll call. "Listen up," he says in front of the men. "The company has been assigned cleaning duties in the south yard. Douglas, you are needed at the depot and Smith, at the Mess. By the way Johnson, your mother died yesterday: report to the Captain." Later that day, the Captain says to the Sergeant: "Sarge, that was a pretty harsh way to break the news to Johnson. Next time, be a bit more tactful when things like this happen, you know?" The Sergeant nods and says that he will. A few days later the captain receives the sad news that Private Allen's mum died of a heart attack during the night. He sends for the Sergeant and tells him to inform Allen – tactfully – of the tragedy and to send the unfortunate soldier to him. The Sergeant nods, salutes and departs. At the roll call, when all the men are lined up, he pauses for a minute, then says: "Right, listen up! All of you who have a mother, two steps forward! Not so fast, Allen!"

****

A Captain to a Sergeant: "Do you have a couple of smart Majors?" "Yes, I do." "Send them to me. I need to move my furniture around."

A soldier, not noted as being very bright, was sitting at the table, looking at a mug upside-down. A Sergeant came to sit next to him with his lunch and the soldier told him: "I can't drink from this mug. It has no opening." The Sergeant examined the mug and says: "You're right. And besides, it has no bottom either."

****

It was a dark, stormy night. The young soldier was on his first assignment – guard duty. The General stepped out, taking his dog, a healthy-looking, very strong German Shepherd, for a walk. The nervous young soldier snapped to attention, made a perfect salute and shouted: "Sir, good evening, Sir!" The General, out for some relaxation, returned the salute and said, "Good evening, soldier: nice night, isn't it?" Well it wasn't a nice night, as it was raining and the soldier had only the standard coat on while the General had a waterproof overcoat and a pair of gloves, but the Private wasn't going to disagree with the General, so he replied, "Sir, yes, Sir!" The General continued, "You know, there's something about a stormy night that I find soothing: it's really relaxing. Don't you agree?" The soldier didn't really agree, but then the soldier was just a soldier, and responded, "Sir, yes, Sir!" The General, pointing at the dog, said: "This is a German Shepherd, the best type of dog to train. Very intelligent, very sensitive and very faithful." The private glanced at the dog, saluted yet again and said: "Sir, yes, Sir!" The General continued, "I got this dog for my wife." The soldier simply said: "Sir, good trade, Sir!"

****

Four people were travelling in the same carriage on a French train. There was an old, distinguished lady wearing a fur coat and a haughty expression; what was probably her granddaughter, a stunning 20-year-old of *Playboy* calibre; a highly decorated General; and a soldier fresh from boot camp. They spend the time chatting about trivial things, and then entered a very long tunnel. While in the tunnel, the sound of a kiss was distinctly heard, followed by the unmistakable sound of a hand slapping a cheek. Silence followed, as all were lost in their respective thoughts: The old lady was thinking: "Isn't it wonderful that, in this day and age, there are still young people ready to defend young women's honour!" The young woman was thinking: "How strange that he would want to kiss the old hag beside me, when I am available!" The General was thinking. whilst, rubbing his stinging cheek: "I am outraged that any woman could think I would try to sneak a kiss in the dark." The soldier had a big grin on his face and was thinking: "Isn't it great that someone can kiss the back of their own hand, then smack a General in the face and get away with it?"

✳✳✳✳

One October, during a dark and stormy night, the following radio conversation took place off the eastern coast of Canada:

Americans: Please divert your course 15 degrees to the north to avoid a collision. Over.

Canadians: Recommend you divert *your* course 15 degrees to the south to avoid a collision. Over.

Americans: This is the Captain of a US Navy ship. I say again, divert *your* course. Over.

Canadians: No. I say again, you divert *your* course. Over.

Americans: This is the aircraft carrier *USS Lincoln*, the second largest ship in the United States' Atlantic fleet. We are accompanied by three destroyers, three cruisers and numerous support vessels. I demand that you change your course 15 degrees north. That's zero-one-five degrees north or countermeasures will be undertaken to ensure the safety of this ship. Over.

Canadians: This is Rock Point Lighthouse, Newfoundland. Your call.

****

A General visits the infirmary to check on his men. He goes to the first soldier, lying in his bed and asks: "What's your problem, soldier?" "Chronic syphilis, Sir." "I see… And what treatment are you getting?" "Five minutes with the wire brush and dettol each day, Sir." "As it should be! And what's your ambition?" "To get back to the front, Sir." "Good man," says the General, and he goes to the next bed. "What about you? What's your problem, soldier?" "Chronic piles, Sir." "Nasty, that… what treatment are you getting?" "Five minutes with the wire brush and dettol each day, Sir." "What an efficient infirmary this is! And what's your ambition, soldier?" "To get back to the front, Sir." "Good man," says the General, and he goes to the next bed. "What's your problem, soldier?" "Chronic gum disease, Sir." "Unusual… And what treatment are you getting?" "Five minutes with the wire brush and dettol each day, Sir." "This is really a top infirmary! And what is your ambition, soldier?" "To be treated before the other two, Sir!"

****

Officer: "Soldier, do you have change for a tenner?" Soldier: "Yeah, sure, buddy." Officer: "That's no way to address an Officer! Now let's try it again. Soldier, do you have change for a tenner?" Soldier: "Sir, no, Sir!"

****

A soldier serving in Hong Kong got quite upset when his girlfriend wrote to him, breaking off their engagement and asking for her photograph back. Out of spite, the soldier went out and collected all the unwanted photographs of women that he could find from his friends, bundled them all together and sent them back with a note saying, "Regret cannot remember which one is you. Please keep your photo and return the others."

****

A mum catches her son on the doorstep, a backpack on his shoulder. "Fred, where are you off to now?" she asks. "I'm going to join the Army," the son replies. "But you can't! You're my little baby!" "That's all right. I'm going to join the infantry."

****

Two military policemen were chasing a fleeing draftee from the base. The draftee ran into the courtyard of a convent where a nun was seated on a bench beneath a tree quietly reading a book. "Quick, sister; please hide me! I don't want to be drafted and the MPs are chasing me!" he said to her. "OK. Hide under my skirt." The two policemen finally entered the convent and asked the nun if she had seen anyone. "I am sorry, officers. I didn't," she replied. After they left, she told the young boy that the coast was clear. "Thank you, sister!" the boy said, very relieved. Then he felt he'd better give her some kind of compliment as a way to show his appreciation of her sacrifice. "Say," he started, "you have a nice set of legs for a nun!" "Don't get any ideas," the nun growled. "If you reach up a little farther you'll find a set of balls! – I'm not going to be drafted either!"

****

In the canteen: "Pass me the chocolate pudding, would you?" "No way, José!" "And why not?" "It's against regulations to help another soldier to dessert!"

****

An F-16 was flying escort with a B-52 and the pilot was generally making a nuisance of himself by flying rolls and other silly show-off manoeuvres around the lumbering old bomber. Fed up with the smaller plane's antics, the pilot of the B-52 announced on the radio to the F-16: "Anything you can do, I can do better." Not to be outdone, the fighter pilot announced that he would rise to the challenge. "OK, then. Try this." The B-52, however, continued its flight, straight and level, apparently not having changed anything. Perplexed, the fighter pilot asked, "So? What did you do?" The B-52 pilot replied, "We just shut down two engines."

****

During camouflage training in a forest, a soldier is disguised as a tree. Suddenly, just as the visiting General approaches his spot, he starts shouting, lurches forward and jumps up and down a few times while spinning frantically on the spot. "You idiot!" the Officer in charge barks, quite angry at having his otherwise uneventful training disrupted right in front of the General. "Don't you know that by jumping and yelling the way you did, you could have endangered the lives of the entire company?" "Yes Sir," the soldier answered apologetically, brushing away a branch from his brow. "But, if I may say so, I did stand still when a flock of pigeons used me for target practice and shat on my head. And I never moved a muscle when a large dog peed on my lower branches. But when two squirrels ran up the leg of my fatigues and I heard the larger of the two say, 'Let's eat one now and save the other until winter,' I couldn't take any more."

****

A Marine reconnaissance platoon was on patrol when the Corporal noticed a lone Special Forces soldier standing on a hilltop. As an exercise, the Corporal told two of his men to go and take out that man. They promptly ran as fast as they could toward the soldier, who disappeared over the other side of the hill. For the next few minutes, bloody screams were heard and dust flew in the air. Then, as quickly as it had started, the noise stopped and the Special Forces soldier re-appeared on the hilltop. He brushed off his uniform, straightened his beret, crossed his arms and stood there looking at the Marines. The

Corporal, rather pissed off, called for a squad to go and get that arrogant soldier. They promptly ran as fast as they could towards him, and once again he disappeared over the other side of the hill just before the squad reached him. For the next few minutes there were bloody screams and dust flew in the air. Then, as quickly as it had started, the noise stopped and the Special Forces soldier came up on the hilltop. He brushed off his uniform, straightened his beret, crossed his arms and stood there looking at the Marines. This was simply too much for the Corporal. He ordered the rest of his platoon to attack the bloody Special Forces soldier, pretty sure that the supremacy in numbers would ensure victory for his patrol. They all ran up the hill screaming war cries and followed the lone soldier over to the other side of the hill. For many minutes, there were bloody screams and dust flew in the air. It continued and continued. Finally, one lone Marine crawled back to the top of the hill and towards the Corporal, all bloody and feeble, his uniform torn, cuts bleeding all over his body. The Corporal gathered the beaten-up soldier in his arms and heard him say: "Run, Sir: it's a trick. There are two of them!"

****

A soldier is telling his friends that his sister just enlisted, disguising herself as a bloke. "Wait a minute: she'll have to get changed and shower with the other blokes, won't she?" one of his friends points out. "So what?" "Well, won't they find out?" "Probably," replies the soldier with a wink, "but who'll tell?"

****

Two young men join the Army and are soon put on street patrol in a city with a military curfew. They are given instructions to shoot anybody who's on the streets after six o'clock. So one day, they're out at twenty to six when one of them spots a man walking on the other side of the street. He lines up the man in his sights and shoots the man dead. The other soldier is shocked. "What are you doing? It's not six yet!" "I know what I'm doing," replies his companion. "I know where he lives and he wouldn't have made it!"

✳✳✳✳

Four friends in the Army were doing very well indeed – so well that they decided to have a little party before the final exams. Off they went to the local whorehouse and had a wonderful time. When they woke up the following day though, they realized that they had missed the examination by a few hours. Gutted, they went to see their teacher: "Sir, we did have a little pre-exam party yesterday, but nothing much really; only this morning, er, the car blew a tyre. That's why we were late…" one of the friends lied glibly. "Is that so?" asked the teacher. "That's unlucky indeed, especially since your results have been outstanding up until now…" After deliberation with his colleagues, the teacher agreed to let them take the exam in the afternoon. "The problem is that we can't get someone to keep an eye on you while you're sitting the exam, so you'll have to use four separate rooms," they were told. Not believing their luck and amazed that their lie had actually worked, they agreed to the conditions and each entered their own examination room. The first question counted for five points and was ever so easy. Elated, sure of passing the exam, they turned the page on their exam paper to discover that the next question, counting for 95 points, said: "Which tyre?"

****

A private who was going to be courtmartialled asked the lawyer representing him for advice on what to wear. "Wear your shabbiest uniform. Let them think you are sorry and repentant," the lawyer replied. Then he asked a friend the same question, but got the opposite advice. "Don't let them intimidate you. Wear your best uniform, with all the decorations and awards you got." Confused, the man went to his chaplain, told him of the conflicting advice and requested some resolution of the dilemma. "Let me tell you a story," replied the chaplain. "A woman, about to be married, asked her mother what to wear on her wedding night. 'Wear a heavy, long, flannel nightgown that goes right up to your neck.' But when she asked her best friend, she got conflicting advice. 'Wear your most sexy negligee, with a V-neck right down to your navel.'" The private protested: "What does all this have to do with me getting courtmartialled?" The priest replied, "No matter what you wear, you are going to get screwed."

****

A young naval student was being grilled by an old sea Captain: "What would you do if a sudden storm sprang up on the starboard bow?" "Throw out an anchor, Sir," the student replied. "What would you do if another storm sprang up after?" "Throw out another anchor, Sir."

"And if another terrific storm sprang up forward, what would you do then?" asked the Captain. "Throw out another anchor, Sir." "Hold on," said the Captain, holding up his hand. "Where are you getting all these anchors from?" "From the same place you're getting your storms, sir."

****

A Private was brought up before the unit Commanding Officer for a minor offence. "Here's your choice, Private," the CO said. "One month's restriction or 20 days' pay." "All right, Sir," said the bright soldier, "I'll take the money."

****

The physical training instructor was drilling a platoon of soldiers. "I want every man to lie on his back, put his legs in the air and move them as though he were riding a bicycle," he explained. "Now begin!" After a few minutes, one of the men stopped. "Why did you stop, Smith?" demanded the officer. "I'm freewheeling for a while," said Smith.

****

A young man, freshly promoted to the rank of Second Lieutenant, takes possession of his new office. He lovingly arranges a set of plaques and medals in prominent view on his desk, puts up a full-length mirror, spends some time looking in it and wonders whether his shoulder buttons need another polish. Then a young soldier comes in. Wishing to pass for a hotshot, the Second Lieutenant picks up the phone, waves the soldier to stand at attention and wait. He then starts throwing in the names of a few Generals, hints at a golfing date, whispers the name of, and describes, the amorous behaviour of a fictitious young lady and various other rubbish. This comedy lasts for ten minutes, after which he hangs up and turns his attention to the soldier. "Can I help you, soldier?" "Yes, Sir. I'm here to activate your phone line."

****

An Army brat was boasting about his father to a Navy brat. "My dad is an engineer. He can do everything. Do you know the Alps?" "Yes," said the Infantry brat. "My dad built them." Then the naval kid spoke: "And do you know the Dead Sea?" "Yes." "Well," said the naval kid, "it was my dad who killed it!"

****

During a training exercise, a Commanding Officer's jeep got stuck in mud. The CO, seeing some men lounging around nearby, asked them to help him get unstuck. "Sorry, Sir," said one of the loafers, "but we've been classified dead and the umpire said we couldn't contribute in any way." The CO turned to his driver and said, "Go and drag a couple of those dead bodies over here and throw them under the wheels to give us some traction."

****

A soldier arrives in a small town a bit late: in fact, just after a whole infantry platoon. He cannot find a free hotel room, until a manager takes pity on his tired state and tells him: "Well, I may have something. There is this guy who comes here every time his company stops by and he always sleeps in the same room. He's snoring so much we have to put him apart from the other tenants, but there's a spare bed in his room." "That's fine: I'll take it," says the soldier, relieved. "But what about the snoring? Let me tell you, this man snores very loudly!" "I'll deal with the snoring, trust me." The manager leads the soldier to the room. Indeed, the guy's snores can be heard two corridors away. The soldier thanks the manager and enters the room. The following morning, he goes to pay the bill. "So, did you have a good night's sleep after all?" the manager sneers. "Never better: you run a very good hotel," the soldier replies. "How did you manage to sleep through the snoring?" the manager asks, baffled. "The guy didn't snore!" "How come?" "It's quite simple," the soldier explained. "Just before going to bed I woke him up, kissed him on the cheek and said, 'Goodnight, beautiful.' He spent the whole night awake watching me."

****

A British pilot gets shot down behind enemy lines. He wakes up in a German hospital, his uniform gone, with a funny feeling in his left leg. A German doctor comes to his bed and says: "I am a doctor before I am a German, and I will treat you with the respect to which any patient is entitled. I must tell you, however, that it is quite possible we'll have to amputate your left leg." The pilot is shocked, but manages to say: "Thank you for your kindness, doctor, and for agreeing to treat me although I am an enemy." He pauses, then says: "Do you think it would be possible to send my leg back to my family in England?" The doctor is a bit surprised by this request, but he agrees. Unfortunately, a month later, the second leg has to go, too, and again the pilot asks him to send it to England. The doctor agrees. Another month goes by and he is forced to admit to himself that the pilot's right arm will soon have to come off. He breaks the news very gently to him and is not surprised to hear that the pilot would like his arm to be shipped home with the rest of his bits. The doctor complies, but, when it comes to the time for the right arm to come off, he is accompanied to the unfortunate pilot's bedside by two German security officers. "So this is the pilot who gets his arms and legs sent to England," one of them says. "Tell me… you're not trying to escape, are you?"

****

After a briefing on land mines, the Captain asked for questions. An intrepid solder raised his hand and asked: "If we do happen to step on a mine, Sir, what do we do?" "Normal procedure, soldier, is to jump 200 feet in the air and scatter oneself over a wide area."

****

Why did King Kong join the Army? He wanted to know about gorilla warfare.

****

Things to do to have the military psychiatric nurses worry over your case:

Jam tiny marshmallows up your nose and try to sneeze them out while on parade.

Use one credit card to pay off another credit card bill, then say you are under stress from the military life.

When one of your roommates says, "Have a nice day!" tell them you have other plans and remind them you are in the Army to die.

During your next roll-call, sneeze and then loudly suck the phlegm back down your throat.

Find out what a frog in a gun barrel really looks like.

Make a list of things you have done in your life and a list of the people you have ever met, then pin them on the wall and shoot them repeatedly.

Dance naked in front of the flagpole on the Winter Solstice.

Put your uniform on backwards, then go to breakfast as if nothing was wrong.

Thumb through *Gun Monthly*, making little cooing noises.

Drive your tank in reverse.

On parade, drop a rabbit on the ground and stop to admire its fluffy coat for 15 minutes, dragging the other conscripts around you.

****

The five most dangerous things you can hear in the Army:

1. A Private saying, "I learned this in Basic…"
2. A Sergeant saying, "Trust me, Sir…"
3. A Second Lieutenant saying, "Based upon my experience…"
4. A Captain saying, "I was just thinking…"
5. A Warrant Officer chuckling, "Watch this shit…"

Hard &
Soft(ware)

Jokes for
computers

A computer programmer was out walking one day when a frog called out to him and said: "If you kiss me, I'll turn into a beautiful princess." Delighted with his find, he bent over, picked up the frog and put it in his pocket. The frog spoke up again and said: "If you kiss me and turn me back into a beautiful princess, I will stay with you for one week." The computer programmer took the frog out of his pocket, smiled at it and returned it again. The frog then cried out: "If you kiss me and turn me back into a princess, I'll stay with you for one week and do *anything* you want." Again the computer programmer took the frog out, smiled at it and put it back into his pocket. Finally, the frog asked: "What's the matter with you? I've told you I'm a beautiful princess, that I'll stay with you for a week and do anything you want. Why won't you kiss me?" The computer programmer said: "Look, I'm a computer programmer. I don't have time for a woman in my life: but a talking frog – now that's cool."

****

Three software engineers were in the toilet, standing at the urinals. The first engineer finished and walked over to wash his hands. He then proceeded to dry them very carefully, using paper towel after paper towel and ensuring that his hands were completely dry. Turning to the other two engineers, he explained, "At Hughie Pickering, we are trained to be extremely thorough." He then began to check the fit of his suit. The second engineer finished his task at the urinal and, in his turn, proceeded to wash his hands. He used a single paper towel and made sure that he dried his hands using every available portion of it. He turned and said, "At Adomo, not only are we trained to be extremely thorough, but also extremely efficient." He then started grooming his hair in the mirror. The third engineer, rather peeved, finished his business and walked straight for the door, shouting over his shoulder: "At Affel, we don't pee on our hands."

****

Macronought today announced the release of JoeBloogs Operating System™, especially targeted at British thirtysomething yobboes, yuppies and club-goers. The operating system, commercialized with the motto "an OS for the mates", doesn't have a spreadsheet, a database program or even a word processor, but it can keep track of the football season, lists the best pubs between Inverness and Dover and can even order curry and beer at the click of a mouse.

****

The new aggressive office jargon:

Blamestorming – Sitting around in a group discussing why a deadline was missed or a project failed and who was responsible.

Body Nazis – Hardcore exercise and weightlifting fanatics who look down on anyone who doesn't work out obsessively.

Chainsaw Consultant – An outside expert brought in to reduce the employee headcount, leaving the top brass with clean hands.

Cube Farm – An office filled with cubicles.

Ego Surfing – Scanning the Net, databases, print media and so on, looking for references to one's own name.

Elvis Year – The peak year of something's popularity: *Survivor*'s Elvis Year was 1993.

404 – Someone who is clueless, from the World Wide Web error message "404 Not Found", meaning the requested document couldn't be located: "Don't bother asking him, he's 404."

Mouse Potato – The on-line generation's answer to the couch potato.

Ohnosecond – That minuscule fraction of time in which you realize you've just made a big mistake.

Prairie Dogging – Something loud happens in a cube farm, as people's heads pop up over the walls to see what's going on.

SITCOM – Stands for Single Income, Two Children, Oppressive Mortgage.

Stress Puppy – A person who thrives on being stressed-out and whiny.

Tourists – Those who take training classes just to take a vacation from their jobs – "We had three serious students in the class; the rest were tourists."

Uninstalled – Euphemism for being fired.

Xerox Subsidy – Euphemism for swiping free photocopies from a workplace.

****

Why are computers like women?

Nobody, however long they work with one, understands their internal
   logic.

Even your smallest mistakes are immediately, permanently committed
   to memory for future reference.

The native language used to communicate with other computers is
   incomprehensible to everyone else.

The message "Bad command or file name" is about as informative as,
   "If you don't know why I'm mad at you, then I'm certainly not
   going to tell you."

As soon as you make a commitment to one, you find yourself
   spending half your pay cheque on accessories for it.

✱✱✱✱

Software magnate Jim Portal has finally died and Satan greets him.
"Welcome, Mr Portal, we've been waiting for you," he purrs. "You've
been a naughty boy, flooding the world with version after version of
software that didn't work and not permitting any other software to
exist. You are now in Hell and this will be your home for all eternity."
Satan eyes Jim Portal and resumes his welcome speech: "But you're
lucky, because I am in a good mood today and I will present to you
three Hells for you to choose to be locked up in." Satan takes Jim to a
huge lake of fire in which millions of poor souls are tormented and
tortured. He then takes him to a massive amphitheatre where
thousands of people are chased about and devoured by starving,
nightmarish creatures. Finally, he takes Jim to a tiny room in which, to

Jim's delight, there is a PC and, next to it, a cup of coffee. Without hesitation, Jim says: "I'll take this option." "Fine," says Satan, locking up Jim in the room. Outside, his second-in-command is waiting for him to process the next unfortunate soul. "So he chose this room, master, as you predicted," the aide says. "But I don't understand. You gave him quite a nice room, and with a PC, too…" "Ah, but you see, this is no ordinary PC," Satan sniggers. "The Control, Alte and Delete keys are missing and it's running Windows 95!"

****

Your computer is lying to you.

It says: "Press Any Key."
It means: "Press any key you like, but I'm not moving."

It says: "Fatal Error. Please contact technical support quoting error no. 1A4-2546512430E."
It means: "… where you will be kept on hold for ten minutes, only to be told some crap that will hide the fact they can't understand a word I say either."

It says: "Installing program to C:\…"
It means: "…. and I'll also be writing 200 megabytes of files into various directories and you'll NEVER find them."

It says: "Please insert disk 11."
It means: "Because I know darn well there are only ten disks."

It says: "Please Wait…"
It means: "… Indefinitely."

It says: "Directory does not exist…"
It means: "… any more. Whoops."

It says: "The application caused an error. Choose Ignore or Close."
It means: "… Makes no difference to me, you're still not getting your work back."

✳✳✳✳

The Ultimate Computer had finally been built and, after making sure that the intensive indoor tests all proved 100 per cent positive, the Ultimate Computer was presented to the CEO. The engineer stepped forward to give his prepared demo. "This," he said, "is the Ultimate Computer. It will give an intelligent answer to any question you may care to ask it." The CEO, amused, asked: "Where is my father?" After an infinitesimal pause, the super computer answer comes through the laser printer: "Your father is fishing off the coast of Florida." The COE's face falls. "Actually, my father is dead. He died five years ago," he says, in a tone suggesting he is not amused any more. The engineer gulps and mutters: "You should re-phrase the question – make it more precise. That might produce a correct answer this time." The CEO frowns and says: "All right. Where is my mother's husband?" There is a small pause again and the printer spits out the answer to the second question: "Your mother's husband is dead. However, your father is still fishing off the coast of Florida."

✳✳✳✳

New PC software error messages:

Smash forehead on keyboard to continue.

File not found. Should I fake it? (Y/N)

Runtime Error 6D at 417A:32CF: Incompetent User.

Enter any 11-digit prime number to continue.

Press any key to continue or any other key to quit.

Press any key except... no, *no, no, not that one*!

Press Ctrl-Alt-Del now for IQ test.

Close your eyes and press escape three times.

Bad command or file name! Go stand in the corner.

This will end your current session. Do you want to play another game?

CONGRESS.SYS Corrupted: Re-boot Washington D.C. (Y/N)?

Windows message: "Error saving file! Format drive now? (Y/Y)"

BREAKFAST.SYS halted... Cereal port not responding.

✳✳✳✳

The librarian noticed a young man sitting in front of a computer, staring at the screen, his arms across his chest. After 15 minutes, he realized that the young man hadn't changed his position and was still there, doing nothing, staring blankly at the screen. Puzzled, he went to him and asked: "May I help you?" "It's about time!" he answered, "I pressed the Help button over 20 minutes ago!"

****

A woman had been married three times and protested that she was still a virgin. Somebody asked her how that could be possible. "Well," she said. "The first time I married an octogenarian and he died before we could consummate the marriage. The second time I married a naval officer and war broke out on our wedding day. The third time I married a PC Operating System programmer and he just sat on the edge of the bed and kept telling me how good it was going to be."

****

Information age proverbs:

Home is where you hang your @.
The e-mail of the species is more deadly than the mail.
A journey of a thousand sites begins with a single click.
You can't teach a new mouse old clicks.
Great groups from little icons grow.
Speak softly and carry a cellular phone.
C:\ is the root of all directories.
Don't put all your hypes in one home page.
Pentium wise; pen and paper foolish.
The modem is the message.

Too many clicks spoil the browse.
The geek shall inherit the earth.
A chat has nine lives.
Don't byte off more than you can view.
Fax is stranger than fiction.

****

A man walks into a Silicon Valley pet store looking to buy a monkey. The owner points towards three identical-looking monkeys in politically-correct, animal-friendly, natural mini-habitats. "The one on the left costs $500," says the owner. "Why so much?" asks the customer. "Because it can program in C," answers the owner. The customer inquires about the next monkey and is told, "That one costs $1,500, because it knows Visual C and Object-Relational technology." The startled man then asks about the third monkey. "That one costs $3,000," answers the store owner. "$3,000!!" exclaims the man. "What can that one do?" The owner replies, "To be honest, I've never seen it do a single thing, but it calls itself a consultant."

****

Dad was happy typing away on his computer and didn't notice his six-year-old daughter sneaking up behind him. Then she turned and ran into the kitchen, squealing to the rest of the family, "I know Daddy's password! I know Daddy's password!" "What is it?" her sister asked eagerly. Proudly she replied, "Asterisk, asterisk, asterisk, asterisk, asterisk!"

****

Alternative Windows slogans:

Double your drive space: Delete Windows!
Windows and DOS: A turtle and its shell.
A computer without Windows is like a fish without a bicycle.
Bang on the left side of your computer to restart Windows.
I still miss Windows, but my aim's getting better.
I'll never forget the first time I ran Windows, but I'm trying.
Out of disk space. Delete Windows? [Y]es, [H]ell Yes!
Windows 3.1: The best solitaire game you can buy.
Windows NT: Insert wallet into Drive A: and press any key to empty.

****

Tech Support: "Tell me, in the bottom left-hand side of the screen, can you see the 'OK' button displayed?" Caller: "Wow. How can you see my screen from there?"

****

Two programmers were walking across their company's campus when one of their colleagues appeared on a brand-new bicycle. "Where did you get such a great bike?" asks the first programmer. 'Well, I was walking along yesterday minding my own business when a beautiful woman rode up on this bike. She threw the bike to the ground, took off all her clothes and said, 'Take what you want.'" The second IT guy nodded approvingly. "Good choice; the clothes probably wouldn't have fitted."

****

Programming today is a race between software engineers striving to build bigger and better idiot-proof programs, and the Universe trying to produce bigger and better idiots. So far, the Universe is winning.

****

Errors are human, but if you really want to screw things up, you need a computer.

****

Beware of computer programmers who carry screwdrivers.

****

The perfect computer has been developed. You just feed in your problems and they never come out again.

****

A computer once beat me at chess, but it was no match for me at kick-boxing.

****

Alpha. Software undergoes alpha testing as a first step in getting user feedback. Alpha is Latin for "doesn't work".

Beta. Software undergoes beta testing shortly before it's released. Beta is Latin for "still doesn't work".

****

A few definitions of computer terms:

Bit: The increment by which programmers slowly go mad.

Branch instruction: Advice from a district office.

Chaining: Method of attaching programmers to desks until output speeds up.

Character density: The number of very weird people in the office, divided by the floorspace.

Checkpoint: Where a programmer draws his salary from.

Computer: A device designed to speed up and automate errors.

Constant: A type of pressure felt by programmers.

Core storage: A receptacle for the centre section of apples.

Debugging: Removing the needles from the haystack.

Default directory: Black hole. Default directory is where all files that you need disappear to.

DSE: Dedicated Solitaire Engine (any PC computer).

Error: Someone else's non-satisfaction with your computer output.

External storage: Wastebasket.

D-word: Four-letter words usual by programmers in a state of confusion.

File: A document that has been saved with an unidentifiable name. It helps to think of a file as something stored in a filing cabinet – except that when you try to remove the file, the cabinet gives you an electric shock and tells you the file format is unknown.

Garbage: Highly aromatic computer output.

Hardware: The parts of a computer which can be kicked.

Help: The feature that assists in generating more questions. When the help feature is used correctly, users are able to navigate through a series of Help screens and end up where they started from without learning anything.

High-speed printer: Wife writing cheques.

Input: Food, whisky, beer, Neurofen.

Input/Output: Information is input from the keyboard as intelligible data and output to the printer as unrecognizable junk.

Internal sort: The stomach, liver and kidneys keep changing positions.

Keyboard: An instrument used for entering errors into a system

Language: A system of organizing and defining error messages

Loop: *See* loop.

Low-order position: The programmers' place in the chain of command.

Machine-independent program: A program which will not run on any machine.

Macro: The last half of an expression: for example "Holy Macro".

Mathematical model: 46-26-38.

Mathematical check: The remuneration received by a mathematical model.

Memory dump: Immediate amnesia after a glimpse of a normal life.

Microcomputer: One millionth of a computer.

Microsecond: The amount of time required for a program to hang.

Null string: The result of a four-hour database search.

Off-line: Failure to pass a sobriety test.

On-line: Full of alcohol, but not drunk.

Output: Four-letter words.

Overflow: The result of drinking too much alcohol.

Parameter: The absolute limit before the secretary yells for help.

Printer: A printer consists of three main parts: the case, the jammed paper tray and the blinking red light.

Program library: An organized collection of obsolete programs.

Reference manual: Object that raises the monitor to eye level. Also used to compensate for that short table leg.

Users: Collective term for those who stare vacantly at a monitor. Users are divided into three types: novice, intermediate and expert.

****

Sex Manual for Tech Nerds

1. Be user-friendly.
2. Take bytes.
3. Fondle joystick.
4. Spread sheet.
5. Fix surge protector.
6. Activate hardware.
7. Insert disk... all the way.
8. Do it until megabytes.
9. Back it up.
10. Eject floppy.

****

Tech Support: "What does the screen say now?" Caller: "It says, 'Hit ENTER when ready'." Tech Support: "Well?" Caller: "How do I know when it's ready?"

****

One of Jim Portal's marketing assistants approached an applicant in a market research panel and said, "Excuse me. If a company made a version of a PC OS which only crashed once a year, would you buy it?" The customer's eyes glistened and he seemed to be making the sign of the cross: "Oh, yes!" The marketing assistant carried on: "… and if they made a version which crashed every five minutes?" The customer glared at him and said, "And what kind of customer do you think I am?" "We've already established that," the guy said. "We're just haggling over the frequency."

****

Windows versions:

Windows 1.0: Good joke, eh?

Windows 2.0: Still funny, isn't it?

Windows 286: Yeah, we're still kidding.

Windows 386: It's wearing thin, so we'll publish something you can actually use real soon.

Windows 3.0: It's finally worth buying!

Windows 3.1: It's finally worth using!

Windows 95: Going boldly where Mac has been for years.

Windows 98: More usable! Less stable!

Windows 98SE: More stable! Less usable!

Windows ME: Less usable *and* less stable!

NT 1.0: Give me more hardware! *Now!*

NT 2.0: Dammit, I said *More hardware*! *Now!*

NT 3.0: Which part of *more hardware* do you not understand?

NT 3.5: With enough hardware, I'd work. Honest.

NT 4.0: Does less than Win98 with twice the hardware at half the speed.

Windows 2K: Works almost as well as Windows 98! Honest!

Windows XP: It just works. Sometimes.

****

If software companies made toasters:

Every time you bought a fresh loaf of bread, you would have to buy a toaster, or at lest renew your licence for it.

Toaster 98 would weigh 15,000 pounds (hence requiring a steel-reinforced worktop), draw enough electricity to power Birmingham, take up 95 per cent of the space in your kitchen and would claim to be the first toaster which lets you control how light or dark you want your toast to be.

This toaster would secretly interrogate your other appliances to find out who made them and send the details back to the parent company.

It would have a protection device that will not let you toast bread.

It will give you advice you don't need, such as: "Don't put your hand in the boiling water, only pasta," and would monitor your behaviour in the kitchen to record your bread-related habits to serve you better.

If your toaster ever caught you running with scissors, the parent company will sue you.

It would have a reset button, the only place worn out on an otherwise shiny toaster.

Everyone would hate toasters, but nonetheless would buy them since most of the good bread only works with their toasters.

✳✳✳✳

One of the main host computers of a very busy internal network went down, bringing down with it half the intranet of the building which depended on it. The network in-house engineer soon gave up and told his boss to call for a specialist. The specialist arrived, had a talk with the engineer, then took one look at the computer and nodded thoughtfully. He then opened his briefcase, produced a small rubber hammer and, his ear stuck to the computer case, hit a spot softly, after which the system made a kind of "Wooosh" noise and restarted straight away. Two days later the office manager received a bill from the consultant for $2,000. Immediately he called the engineer's agency and exclaimed, "Two thousand dollars for fixing that computer? You were only here five minutes! I want the bill itemized!" The next day the new bill arrived. It read, "Tapping computer with hammer: $1. Knowing where to tap: $1,999."

****

A young man comes into the computer store: "I'm looking for a mystery adventure game with lots of graphics: you know – something really challenging." "Well," replied the clerk, "have you tried Windows XP?"

****

Viruses are the bane of modern technology. Here is a list of dangerous new viruses you *don't* want to see spreading:

AIRLINE VIRUS
You're in London, but your data is in Inverness.

TONY BLAIR VIRUS

It doubles the files on your hard drive while stating it is decreasing the number of files; increases the cost of your computer; taxes its CPU to maximum capacity and then uses Quicken to access your bank accounts and deplete your balances.

BILL GATES VIRUS

This dominant strain searches for desirable features in all other viruses via the Internet. It then either engulfs the competing viruses or removes their access to computers until they die out.

DIET VIRUS

Allows your hard drive to lose weight by eliminating the FAT table.

DISNEY VIRUS

Everything in the computer goes goofy.

ELVIS VIRUS

Your computer gets fat, slow and lazy and then self-destructs, only to re-surface at shopping malls and service stations across rural America.

FREUDIAN VIRUS

Your computer becomes obsessed with its own motherboard, or it becomes very jealous of the size of your friend's hard disk.

LORENA BOBBITT VIRUS

It turns your hard disk into a 3.5-inch floppy.

MISSING VIRUS

Virus '98 is promised for initial Beta release by the second quarter of this year, but recent court actions by the Federal government have cast doubt on the parent company's ability to incorporate this virus into the main OS in a seamless manner.

POLITICALLY CORRECT VIRUS

Never calls itself a "virus", but instead refers to itself as an "electronic micro-organism".

SPICE GIRL VIRUS

Has no real function, but makes a pretty desktop.

STAR TREK VIRUS

Invades your system in places where no virus has gone before.

TEENAGER VIRUS

Your PC stops every few seconds to ask for money.

X-FILES VIRUS

All your icons start shape-shifting.

TOBACCO INDUSTRY VIRUS

It contends that there is no reliable scientific evidence that viruses can harm your computer or that it targets adolescent computer users.

****

A collection of "Ass" emotions

(_E=mc2_) A smart ass.

(_$_) Money coming out of his ass.

(_!_) A regular "nice" ass.

(__!__) A large ass.

(!) A tight ass.

(_._) A flat ass.

(_^_) A bubbly ass.

(_*_) A sore ass.

(_!__) A lop-sided ass.

{_!_} A squishy ass.

(_o_) An ass that's been around.

(_O_) And more…

(_x_) Kiss my ass.

(_X_) Get off my ass.

(_zzz_) A tired ass.

(_o^o_) A wise ass.

(_13_) An unlucky ass.

****

Sure signs that your co-worker is a hacker :

You told him off once and your next phone bill was for £20,000.

He's won the Readers' Digest sweepstakes three years running.

When asked for his phone number, he gives it in hex.

Seems strangely calm whenever the office LAN goes down.

Somehow manages to get Sky Sports on his PC at work.

Mumbled, "Oh, puh-leeez" 95 times during the movie *The Net*.

Massive £40,000 contribution to the ritual Christmas booze trip to Calais made in one-cent increments.

His video dating profile lists "public-key decryption" among turn-ons.

When his computer starts up, you hear, "Good morning, Mr President."

You hear him murmur, "Let's see you use that credit card now, bitch!"

✳✳✳✳

How many Internet mail list subscribers does it take to effect the changing of a light bulb?

1331 – one to change the light bulb and to post to the mail list that the light bulb has been changed.

14 – to share similar experiences of changing light bulbs and how the light bulb could have been changed differently.

7 – to caution about the dangers of changing light bulbs.

27 – to point out spelling/grammar errors in posts about changing light bulbs.

53 – to flame the spell-checkers.

156 – to write to the list administrator complaining about the light bulb discussion and its inappropriateness to this mail list.

41 – to correct spelling in the spelling/grammar flames.

109 – to post that this list is not about light bulbs and to please take this email exchange to alt.lite.bulb.

203 – to demand that cross-posting to alt.grammar, alt.spelling and alt.punctuation about changing light bulbs be stopped.

111 – to defend the posting to this list saying that we all use light bulbs and therefore the posts **are** relevant to this mail list.

306 – to debate which method of changing light bulbs is superior, where to buy the best light bulbs, what brands of light bulb work best for this technique and what brands are faulty.

27 – to post URLs where one can see examples of different light bulbs.

14 – to post that the URLs were posted incorrectly, and to post corrected URLs.

3 – to post about links they found from the URLs that are relevant to this list which makes light bulbs relevant to this list.

33 – to concatenate all posts to date, then quote them including all headers and footers, and then add "Me Too".

12 – to post to the list that they are unsubscribing because they cannot handle the light bulb controversy.

19 – to quote the "Me Too's" to say, "Me Three."

4 – to suggest that posters request the light bulb FAQ.

1 – to propose new alt.change.lite.bulb newsgroup.

47 – to say this is just what alt.physic.cold_fusion was meant for: leave it here.

143 – votes for alt.lite.bulb.

****

A trucker is driving a trailer loaded with computer equipment on the highway near Silicon Valley when he decides to stop for a bite to eat.

He slows down and pulls over at a roadside café which has a sign outside saying: "Non-computer geeks only. If you *are* a computer geek, enter at your own risk." Finding this a bit strange, the trucker goes in and sits at the bar, where a suspicious barman looks him up and down and says: "You're sure you're not a computer geek?" "Hell no. I'm a truck driver." The barman leans over the bar and sniffs him unceremoniously. "You smell like one," the barman accuses. "Well, my trailer's full of computer equipment, that would be why," the trucker replies quickly, starting to feel a tad freaked out. The barman stares at him in the eye for a few seconds and then apparently decides the trucker is telling the truth and serves him lunch. While the trucker is having his lunch, a guy wearing an Apple hat, a calculator-wristwatch and carrying a laptop enters the bar, obviously preoccupied with some difficult programming problem. The barman silently picks up a shotgun from behind the bar, walks around and coldly shoots the geek down. While a couple of waitresses are grumpily disposing of the body, the barman explains that these things happen all the time round these parts. "Oh yeah," he says to the trucker. "Disposing of computer geeks is a state law here. There's just too many of them in Silicon Valley: we need to control the population, you know?" Puzzled, the trucker pays for his food and heads off. Unfortunately, his lunch makes him drowsy and soon he finds himself with his trailer in the ditch, doors open, computer gear on the tarmac. There are a lot of people wearing suits and glasses hurriedly grabbing computers, monitors and keyboards. Remembering the barman's words, he reaches for his shotgun and starts shooting computer geeks, too. He's starting to have fun when a patrol car stops and a couple of policemen restrain him. "What's the matter?" the trucker asks. "I thought it was a state law to get rid of computer geeks?" "Oh, it is," one of the policemen says, "but you're not allowed to bait them."

✷✷✷✷

What does a baby computer call his father?
Data.

✷✷✷✷

What is a computer's first sign of old age?
Loss of memory.

✷✷✷✷

What happened when the computer fell on the floor?
It slipped a disk.

✷✷✷✷

How many Microsoft engineers does it take to screw in a light bulb?
None. They just re-define the status of darkness.

✷✷✷✷

How do you tell an experienced hacker from a novice?
The latter thinks there are 1,000 bytes in a kilobyte, while the former is sure there are 1,024 metres in a kilometre.

****

Why do computer scientists make such lousy lovers?
Because they always want to do the job faster than before. And when they do, they say the performance has improved.

****

WARNING: There is a new virus called Viagra! It turns your 3.5-inch floppy into a hard drive!

****

How many Pentium designers does it take to screw in a light bulb?
Approximately 1,999,042,740,172.23554177896 – but that's close enough for non-technical people.

****

One on One

5

Jokes in a
line or *two*

What did the sign on the door of the brothel say?
Beat it – 'cos we're closed.

Why were glow-in-the-dark condoms invented?
To enable gay people to play *Star Wars*.

Why is air a lot like sex?
Because it's no big deal until you aren't getting any.

Why did the snowman drop his trousers?
He heard the snowblower coming.

What's another name for pickled bread?
Dill-dough.

What do you do with 365 used condoms?
Melt them down, make a car tyre and call it a "Goodyear".

Why is sex just like KFC?
You start with breast, work your way down the thigh, and all you're ever left with is a greasy box to put your bone in!

What do you call a lesbian dinosaur?
Lickalottapus.

****

Chat-up lines to make her laugh:

I'll cook you dinner if you cook me breakfast.

Can I have your phone number? I don't seem to be able to find my own.

You must be jelly, because jam doesn't shake like that.

I definitely go down on the first date: how about you?

If you think you might regret this in the morning, we can always sleep until the afternoon.

Do you have a mirror in your pocket? Because I could see myself in your underwear.

I'm a necrophiliac – how good are you at playing dead?

Do you know why you should masturbate with these two fingers? Because they're mine.

I hope you know CPR, because you take my breath away!

Excuse me: do you want to screw, or should I apologize?

Do you want to go out for a coffee and sex? What, you don't like coffee?

Look at you: all those curves and me with no brakes.

Let's go back to my place and get something straight between us.

Have you ever tried those prickly condoms?

Can I tickle your belly from the inside?

Do you know what winks and fucks like a beast? [Then wink, you dozy sod!]

Are you free tonight, or is it going to cost me?

Inheriting eighty million Euro doesn't mean a lot when you have a weak heart like me.

If you were a car, I'd buff you up and ride you all over town.

There are 265 bones in the human body. How would you like another one?

Oh, I'm sorry, I thought that was a Braille name-tag.

If you cut your arms off, you'd look just like Venus de Milo.

I'd really love to screw your brains out, but it looks like someone beat me to it.

I'm a birdwatcher and you seem to have some of the characteristics of the Big-Breasted Bed Thrasher... I'd like to do more research.

Why don't you sit on my lap and let us see what pops up?

If I could re-arrange the alphabet, I'd put U and I together.

I may not be Fred Flintstone, but I bet I can make your bed rock.

Excuse me, is that dress felt? Would you like it to be?

I wish you were a Postman Pat van outside Tesco's, because then I could ride you all day for a quid.

I like every bone in your body, especially mine.

I'm pretty sure I could fall madly in bed with you.

Nice shoes. Wanna fuck?

If I gave you sexy underwear, would there be anything in it for me?

Excuse me, ma'am, do you go down on strangers? No? Well, allow me to introduce myself.

If you've lost your virginity, can I have the box it came in?

Do you sleep on your stomach? Do you mind if I do?

Let's go to my place and do all the things I'll tell everyone we did anyway.

Screw me if I'm wrong, but do you want to kiss me?

If your left leg was Christmas and your right leg was New Year, could I spend some time between the holidays?

Forget that. Playing doctor is for kids. I prefer to play gynaecologist.

Is that a Tic-Tac in your trousers or are you just pleased to see me?

Nice dress – can I talk you out of it?

Is it hot in here or is it just you?

You must be from the Carribean, because Jamaican me crazy.

Want to play "Down at the Fair"? That's where you sit on my face and I try to guess your weight.

You may not be the best-looking girl here, but beauty is only a light switch away.

Do you know the difference between a hamburger and a blowjob? You don't? Wanna do lunch?

Hey baby, do you want to see something really swell?

Do you believe in love at first sight, or should I walk past again?

The word of the day is "legs". Let's go back to my place and spread the word.

Screw me if I'm wrong, but is your name Sirenija?

Do you wash your underwear with Windex? Because I can really see myself in it.

I was just thinking that your outfit would look great in a crumpled heap on my bedroom floor tomorrow morning.

You know what would look really good on you? Me.

Do you like short love affairs? I hate them. I've got all weekend.

That shirt is very becoming on you, but if I were on you, I'd be coming, too.

You've got the whitest teeth I've ever come across.

****

What was the smartest thing that ever came out of a woman's mouth?
Einstein's dick.

What do you call a lesbian from Canada?
A Klondyke!

How is a woman like a laxative?
They both irritate the shit out of you.

What do a woman and a computer have in common?
Both can take a 3.5-inch floppy.

What's worse than a male chauvinist pig?
A woman that won't do what she's told.

Why do women rub their eyes when they wake up?
Because they don't have balls to scratch.

What do you call a virgin lying on a waterbed?
A cherry float.

What do you call a lesbian from India?
Minjeeta.

What's hairy on the outside, wet and slimy on the inside, begins with a "C" and ends in "T"?
A coconut.

Why did God give men penises?
So they'd have at least one way to shut a woman up.

Why do women paratroopers always wear tampons?
So they don't whistle as they make their way down.

****

What's the difference between a woman with PMT and a pit bull?
Lipstick.

Why do most women pay more attention to their appearance than improving their minds?
Because most men are stupid, but not many are blind.

Why do women like to have sex in the dark?
They can't stand seeing a man have a good time.

What term describes a woman paralyzed from the waist down?
Married.

Why do men die before their wives?
They want to.

What does a 75-year-old woman have between her breasts that a 25-year-old doesn't?
Her navel.

What's a wife?
An attachment you screw on the bed to get the housework done.

What happened to the guy who figured out what it was with women?
He died laughing before he could tell anybody.

Why are hangovers better than women?
Hangovers will go away eventually.

Why do women have tits?
So men will talk to them.

What do the small bumps around a woman's nipples represent?
Braille for "Suck here".

****

What's the difference between your wife and your job?
After five years your job will still suck.

Why did God make Man first?
He didn't want a woman looking over his shoulder.

Why don't women need to wear watches?
There's a clock on the stove!

What's six inches long, two inches wide and drives women wild?
Cash.

What do a woman and a washing machine have in common?
They both drip when they're fucked!

Why did the woman cross the road?
Who cares? How did she get out of the kitchen?

How many women does it take to change a light bulb?
Who cares? Let her cook in the dark!

What is the difference between a woman and a washing machine?
You can bung your load in a washing machine and it won't call you a week later.

If your wife keeps coming out of the kitchen to nag you, what have you done wrong?
Made her chain too long.

What's the difference between a pregnant woman and a light bulb?
You can unscrew a light bulb.

Why can't you trust women?
How can you trust something that bleeds for five days and doesn't die?

Why do women have periods?
They deserve them.

****

What's the difference between your pay cheque and your penis?
You don't have to beg your wife to make her blow your salary!

What's the difference between your wife and a wheelie bin?
You only need to take a wheelie bin out once a week.

Why are women's feet small?
So they can stand closer to the sink.

How do you make your girlfriend scream out loud while you're having sex?
Phone her to let her know what she's missing!

What's the ultimate in sexual rejection?
Your hand falls asleep while you're masturbating!

Have you heard about the new super-sensitive condoms?
They hang around and talk to the woman after you've rolled over, farted and fallen asleep.

Who's the world's greatest athlete?
The man who gets gold and silver medals in the masturbation contest.

Why didn't the man report his stolen credit card?
The thief was spending less than his wife.

Why haven't we sent a woman to the moon?
It doesn't need cleaning.

What did the banana say to the vibrator?
What are you shaking for? It's me she's going to eat!

Why do men pay more for car insurance? Women don't get blowjobs
while they're driving.

****

What do bungee-jumping and prostitutes have in common?
They both cost too much for an afternoon, and if the rubber breaks, you're fucked!

How do you know if you have a high sperm count?
If the girl has to chew before she swallows.

How do you make two kilos of fat look good?
Stick a nipple on top.

Why are Wonderbras so called?
When a woman takes one off, you wonder where her tits went!

Your dog is barking to be let in the back door and your wife is barking to be let in the front door. Which do you let in first?
The dog – once he's in, at least he shuts up!

What's the definition of a "yankee"?
It's like a "quickie", but you do it alone!

What do you call two lesbians in a canoe?
Fur traders.

How do you know when your wife is dead?
Your sex life remains the same but your dirty clothes basket overflows.

Did you hear about the new lesbian leather shoes?
They're called Dikes, have an extra-long tongue and you can get them off with only one finger!

Why do women cease menstruating when they begin the menopause?
They need all the blood for their varicose veins!

How do you turn a fox into an elephant?
Marry it.

What tells you you are getting old?
When your dreams stay dry and your farts get wet!

****

What's better than roses on your piano?
Tulips on your organ.

What did Cinderella do when she got to the ball?
She choked!

What do you do if your dishwasher stops working?
Shout at her.

What do parsley and pubic hair have in common?
You push them both aside and keep on eating!

What do a toilet seat and a pussy have in common?
They both feel good, but you wonder who was there before you.

Do you know what the *Oxford English Dictionary* definition of a
menstrual period is?
A bloody waste of fucking time.

Why don't witches wear panties when flying on their broomsticks?
Better traction.

Why do women pierce their belly-buttons?
Gives them somewhere to hang air freshener.

How did Pinocchio discover he was made of wood?
His hand caught alight!

What's the difference between pussy and apple pie?
You can eat mom's apple pie!

What is the difference between a clever midget and a venereal disease?
One's a cunning runt...

****

What do tightrope-walking and a blowjob from your granny have in common?
You don't look down.

What do women and police cars have in common?
They both make a lot of noise to let you know they're coming.

What is better than a cold Bud?
A warm bush.

What's the difference between a lawyer and a prostitute?
A prostitute will stop screwing with you when you're dead!

Why do women have two per cent more brainpower than cows?
So that when you pull their tits they won't shit on the floor.

What do a virgin and a balloon have in common?
One prick and it's all over.

Why can a prostitutes make more money than a drug dealer?
Because she can wash and re-sell her crack.

What do you do if your girlfriend starts smoking?
Slow down and lubricate.

What's the difference between a woman and a fridge? A fridge doesn't make a squelching noise when you pull your meat out!

What do women and linoleum floors have in common?
You lay them right the first time and you can walk all over them for 20 years!

What is it when a man talks dirty to a woman?
Sexual harassment.

What is it when a woman talks dirty to a man?
Two euro a minute.

****

What is the definition of making love?
Something a woman does while a man fucks her.

What's the difference between a whore and a bitch?
Whores sleep with everyone at the party and bitches sleep with everyone at the party apart from you.

What does the sperm clinic say to donors when they leave?
Thanks for coming.

What's the definition of macho?
Jogging home from your own vasectomy.

How do you have sex with a fat bird?
Roll her in flour and screw the wet bit.

What do a gynaecologist and a pizza man have in common?
They can both smell it, but they can't eat it.

How many men does it take to open a beer bottle?
What the hell? It should be open when she brings it to you!

Why is the space between a woman's breasts and hips called a waist?
Because there's enough room for another pair of tits in there.

What do a fat bird and a moped have in common?
They're both great fun to ride until your mates catch you.

How many newspapers can a woman hold between her legs?
One *Post*, two *Globes* and as many *Times* as you can.

What's the difference between pink and purple?
Grip!

****

What do you call a lesbian with fat fingers?
Well-hung.

Where do homosexuals park?
In the rear.

Why do women have two holes so close together?
If you miss the pink you can go for the brown!

What do you call haemorrhoids on a homosexual?
Speed bumps.

What's the difference between a sumo wrestler and a feminist?
A sumo wrestler has a feminine side.

What's the smallest hotel known to man?
A pussy – leave the bags on the outside.

What do you do in case of fall-out?
Put it back in and take shorter strokes!

What do you call three lesbians in bed together?
Menage à twat.

What's the difference between a man buying a lottery ticket and a man arguing with his wife?
The man buying the ticket at least has a one in 16 million chance of winning!

How can you tell a hardcore lesbian bar?
Even the pool table has no balls.

What's the difference between a bandleader and a gynaecologist?
A gynaecologist sucks his fingers…

How can you tell the head nurse?
She's got dirty knees!

****

What's the late-night difference between a bachelor and a married man?
A bachelor comes home, sees what's in the refrigerator and goes to
bed. A married man comes home, sees what's in the bed and goes to
the refrigerator.

Why do brides always wear white?
Aren't all kitchen appliances that colour?

How do you confuse a female archaeologist?
You give her a used tampon and ask her what period it's from.

How do you tell when an auto mechanic has just had sex?
One of his fingers is clean.

Why do women wear black underwear?
Mourning – for the stiff they buried the night before.

✳✳✳✳

Have you heard about the new mint-flavored birth control pill for
women that they take immediately before sex?
They're called Pre-dickamints.

What's the difference between parsley and pussy?
Nobody eats parsley.

What's the difference between mad cow disease and PMS?
Nothing.

What is the difference between an ice hockey game and a school reunion?
At a hockey game you see fast pucks...

How can you tell when your girlfriend wants you?
You put your hand down her underwear and it feels like you're feeding a horse.

Why are women like tyres?
You can always find a spare.

****

What's good about having a homeless girlfriend?
You can drop her off wherever you want!

Why did God give women arms?
Do you know how long it would take to lick a bathroom clean?

What do homosexuals and ambulances have in common?
They both load from the back and go whoo-whoo!

What's the difference between a hangover and a woman?
A hangover will go away eventually.

What do being in the military and getting a blowjob have in common?
The closer you get to discharge, the better it gets.

What's the definition of eternity?
The time between when you cum and she leaves.

Did you hear about the new gay sitcom?
It's called *Leave It, It's Beaver*.

Why is a laundrette a bad place to pick up chicks?
If she can't afford a washing machine, she'll never be able to support you.

Did you hear there's a new PC word for lesbian?
Vagitarian.

What's the difference between sin and shame?
It's a sin to put it in, but it's a shame to pull it out.

Did you know that 70 per cent of the gay population were born that way?
The other 30 per cent were sucked into it.

****

How does a man show he's planning for the future?
He buys two cases of beer instead of one.

Why do doctors slap babies' arses as soon as they're born?
To knock the penises off the clever ones.

How many men does it take to tile a bathroom?
Two – if you slice them thinly enough.

What's the difference between a cream cracker and a lesbian?
One's a snack cracker...

What has eight arms and an IQ of 60?
Four guys watching a football match.

Why do men have holes in their penises?
So their brains can get some oxygen occasionally.

What does it mean when a man is in your bed gasping for breath and calling your name?
You didn't hold the pillow down long enough.

Why do female black widow spiders kill their partners after mating?
To stop the snoring before it starts.

Why do only ten per cent of men make it to Heaven?
Because if they all got there, it would be Hell.

What do husbands and lawn mowers have in common?
They're hard to start in the morning, they belch out noxious odours
and half the time they don't even work.

What does it take for a man to plan a candlelit dinner?
A power failure.

****

Things never to say to an excited, naked man:

I've smoked fatter joints than that.

Wow – and your feet are so big!

Why don't we skip right to the cigarette?

Is that an optical illusion?

Does it come with an air pump?

It's OK: we'll work around it!

Maybe it looks better in natural light.

Maybe if we water it, it'll grow.

But it still works, right?

How sweet: you brought incense.

Can I be honest with you?

Why, oh, why is God punishing me?

Oh no… a flash headache! (giggle and point)

Can I paint a "smiley face" on it?

Why don't we just cuddle?

Only if you get me real drunk first.

This explains your car.

You know, they have surgery to fix that.

Ahhhh, isn't it cute!

Are you cold?

It looks so unused.

It's a good thing you have so many other talents.

Make it dance!

At least this won't take long.

I suppose this makes me the "early bird".

What *is* that?

Will it squeak if I squeeze it?

I never saw one like that before.

So this is why you're supposed to judge people on personality.

****

Why is psychoanalysis quicker for men than for women?
When it's time for regression, men are already there.

What do theme parks and Viagra have in common?
They both make you wait hours for a two-minute ride.

How do men sort their dirty clothes?
"Dirty" and "dirty-but-wearable".

What did the elephant say to the naked man?
How do you breathe through something that small?

Why don't men give their penises female names?
Because they don't want a woman running their life.

What's the difference between a man and ET?
ET phoned home.

What do Santa's female reindeer do on Christmas Eve while the male reindeer pull his sleigh and deliver presents?
They head into town to blow a few bucks.

Why don't little girls fart?
Because they don't get arseholes until they're married.

What do a Rubik's cube and a penis have in common?
They both get harder the longer you play with them.

How do you ruin a man's ego?
By asking, "Is it in yet?"

✳✳✳✳

Why does it take one million sperm to fertilize one egg?
None of them bother to stop for directions.

Why is it so difficult to find men who are sensitive, caring and good-looking?
They already have boyfriends.

What's the difference between a singles' bar and a circus?
Clowns don't talk at the circus.

Why do men find it difficult to make eye contact?
Tits don't have eyes.

Why can't women read maps?
Because only the male mind can comprehend the concept of an inch equalling a mile.

What do a clitoris, an anniversary and a toilet have in common?
Men will always miss them.

What do you get if you cross a rooster with peanut butter?
A cock that sticks to the roof of your mouth.

Why does a bride smile when she walks down the aisle?
She knows she's given her last blowjob.

Why do women prefer elderly gynaecologists?
Shaky hands!

What's the difference between a new husband and a new dog?
The dog is still excited to see you a year later.

Why don't women blink during foreplay?
They don't have enough time.

Why does a man eating oysters improve a woman's sex life?
Because if he'll eat one of those, he'll eat anything!

****

Which two words clear out a men's changing room quickest?
Nice cock!

Why do penises have a hole in the end?
So men can be open-minded.

What did Adam say to Eve?
"Stand back: I'm not sure how big this thing gets!"

What's the difference between "Oh!" and "Aaah!"?
About two inches.

How many honest, intelligent, caring, sensitive men in the world does it take to do the dishes?
Both of them.

Why is sleeping with a man like a soap opera?
Just when it's getting interesting, it's all over until next time.

What's the sex speed limit?
68, because at 69 you have to turn around.

What must be the lightest thing known to man?
A penis – even a thought can raise it!

What is the difference between a golf ball and a G-spot?
Men will spend hours searching for a golf ball.

How do you know when it's Barbie's period?
You can't find any of your Tic-Tacs!

Why do schools in Kentucky only have driving education classes two days a week?
Because they need their cars for sex education classes for the other three days!

What do you call a guy who never farts in public?
A private tutor.

****

What's the last thing "Tickle Me Elmo" receives before he leaves the factory?
Two test tickles.

What's the difference between a girl snowman and a boy snowman?
Snowballs.

What's the only animal with an arsehole in the middle of its back?
A police horse.

What do bulls do to stay warm on cold days?
Go into the barn and slip into a nice warm Jersey.

Did you hear about the Morning After Pill for men?
It changes your blood type!

What has one hundred balls and screws old ladies?
Bingo.

Why do bunny rabbits have soft sex?
Because they have cotton balls!

How do you describe a "69" in Chinese?
Twocanchew!

What happens when you kiss a canary?
You get chirpes and it can't be tweeted because it's a canarial disease.

Why did God create alcohol?
So ugly people would get to have sex.

How do you make four old ladies swear?
Get a fifth old lady to shout "Bingo!"

What's the difference between oral and anal sex?
Oral sex makes your day; anal sex makes your hole weak.

****

How do you eat a frog?
You put one leg over each ear.

What has two grey legs and two brown legs?
An elephant with diarrhoea.

Did you know they just discovered a new use for sheep in Wales?
Making wool!

What does the female part of a snail say during sex?
Faster, faster, faster!

What happened to the Pope as he went to Mount Olive?
Popeye nearly killed him!

What is "egghead"?
What Mrs Dumpty gives to Humpty.

Why did the Avon Lady walk funny?
Her lipstick.

What is the noisiest thing in the world?
Skeletons bonking on a tin roof.

How do you find a blind man in a nudist colony?
Keep looking – it's not hard.

What's another name for an adolescent rabbit?
A pubic hare.

What did the cannibal do after he dumped his girlfriend?
Wiped his arse.

How do you tell if you have acne?
Blind people can read your face.

****

Why did the lumber truck stop?
To let the lumber jack off.

What do Eskimos get if they sit on ice for too long?
Polaroids.

What's green, slimy and smells like Miss Piggy?
Kermit the Frog's finger.

What's the difference between a toad and a horny toad?
One goes "Gribbit"; the other goes "Grabbit".

What do you call an Amish man with his hand up a horse's arse?
A mechanic.

What do you call a nun with a sex change operation?
A tran-sister.

What's sticky, white and falls from the sky?
The Lord's second cumming!

What did the woman say to the swimming instructor?
"Will I really drown if you take your finger out?"

What do you call a Welsh farmer with a sheep under each arm?
A pimp.

What's brown and sits on a piano stool?
Beethoven's First Movement.

What is the square root of 69?
Ate something.

Why did the woman get thrown out of the riding stable?
She wanted to mount the horse her way.

✳✳✳✳

What do you find in a clean nose?
Fingerprints!

What's the worst bit about a lung transplant?
The first time you cough, it's not your phlegm!

What's bad about being a test tube baby?
You know for sure that your dad was a wanker.

How do you know when a male porn star is in your petrol station?
Just before the petrol tank's full, he pulls out the hose and sprays petrol all over the car.

Why did the rag doll get thrown out of the toy box?
She kept sitting on Pinocchio's face and shouting, "Lie to me, lie to me!"

What do you call a vegetarian with diarrhoea?
A salad shooter.

What's the difference between a Spice Girls video and a porno?
The porno has better music!

What's the biggest crime committed by transvestites?
Male fraud.

What do you get when you cross a male chicken with a flea?
An itchy cock.

What's grey, sits by a bed and takes the piss?
A dialysis machine.

Did you about the two gay men who argued in the bar?
They went outside to exchange blows.

Did you hear the one about the blind circumciser?
He got the sack.

★★★★

Why are eggs frustrated?
They only get laid once, eaten once, and you have to boil them if you want to eat them hard!

Why do walruses go to Tupperware parties?
They hope to find a tight seal.

What's the difference between love and herpes?
Love is not forever.

Why did the washing machine laugh?
Because it was taking the piss out of the knickers!

What did the lesbian frogs say to each other?
We do taste like chicken!

What do the letters "DNA" stand for?
National Dyslexics' Association.

Your family is so poor that when I went over to visit you at your house I stepped on a cigarette butt and your momma said, "Who turned off the heating?"

What would happen if the Founding Fathers had killed cats instead of turkeys?
Americans would be eating pussy every Thanksgiving.

Why did the man put is money in the freezer?
He wanted some cold, hard cash!

What's brown and sticky?
A stick!

How do you know that carrots are good for your eyesight?
Have you ever seen a rabbit wearing glasses?

What do you call a surgeon with eight arms?
A doctopus!

Why do men prefer to take showers rather than baths?
Pissing in a bath is revolting!

★★★★

What do you call kids born in whorehouses?
Brothel sprouts.

Did you know that Cher is re-forming the Spice Girls?
She'll be Old Spice.

Why did the one-handed man cross the road?
To get to the second-hand shop.

How do you know when your cat's finished cleaning itself?
He smokes a cigarette.

What's the definition of trust?
Two cannibals giving each other a blowjob.

What's the difference between a tampon and a cowboy hat?
Cowboy hats are for arseholes.

Did you hear about the streaker who was thinking of retirement?
He decided to stick it out for one more year!

Which meat is cheapest in the USA?
Deer balls – you'll find them under a buck.

Did you hear the one about the constipated mathematician?
He worked it out with a pencil.

Why don't skeletons fight each other?
None of them have the guts!

What did the alien say when he landed in the garden?
Take me to your weeder!

****

More Tea Vicar?

6

Not for the
faint-hearted

A native American Indian went to his father one day because his school was doing a project on how people get their names and where names come from. He first asked, "Father, why was it that you named my first sister Buffalo Grazing?" The chief looked at his son and said, "On the morning after the birth of your first sister, I walked out of the hot, sweaty teepee and I looked around the plains. I saw great beauty around me, and I saw the fields where the graceful buffalo graze peacefully. I hoped that she would know peace like these fine animals, and decided to name her Buffalo Grazing." "That's great," said the son, "and why did you name my other sister Full Moon Shining?" "Well,' said the chief, "on the evening of the birth of your other sister, I walked out of the hot, sweaty teepee and looked around me. It was still dark and the only light came from the moon above. I thought of the light of life that had just been breathed into the little one and decided to name her Full Moon Shining." "That's great, dad," said the boy. And the father looked at him once more, and asked, "But why do you ask, Two Dogs Humping?"

****

A husband and wife went to see a poncey European art movie at their local cinema. It was pretty strong stuff and involved a lot of graphic sex – all in the name of art, of course, nothing porno about it. The husband thought it was great, but the wife was a bit disturbed by the content, particularly by a scene of people masturbating which left nothing to the imagination. As the couple were having a drink afterwards, the wife said to her husband, "You know dear, I find it very difficult to deal with masturbation in the movies," to which the husband replied, "Oh, sorry love, I'll stop doing it then!"

****

Marty was doing some river fishing. A big one bit, and when he fished it out he had a big surprise: it was a goldfish. "Oi, fisherman," said the fish, "if you set me free I'll give you whatever you want. I'm a magic fish and I'll grant you three wishes." "Sounds good to me," thought Marty, "I've got it made now." "OK, then," said Marty. "My first wish is to have a truck full of money." "At your command," said the goldfish. A top-of-the-range truck filled to the brim with cash appeared on the road next to the river; the key appeared in Marty's hand. "My second wish is to have a different top model to sleep with every night of every year." "At your command," said the goldfish, and a diary appeared in Marty's hand with a full schedule of women filled in. "My third wish is for my cock to touch the floor," said Marty. "At your command," said the goldfish, and he cut Marty's legs off.

****

A boy's mother is pregnant, so she has to go off to hospital. The night before she goes, the boy chances upon her in the bathroom and sees hair between her legs. He asks, "What's that, Mummy?" and she tells him, "It's my washcloth, dear." A couple of weeks later the mother is back from hospital, but she had to have her pubic hair shaved during the birth. The boy chances in on her again and notices that her hair has gone. He asks, "What happened to your washcloth, Mummy?" and his mother replies, "I lost it dear." A couple of days later the boy is running through the house shouting "Mummy, I found your washcloth," so his mother stops him and says, "What do you mean, dear?" "I found your washcloth, Mummy," the boy says again. The mother finds this pretty odd, but decides to go along with it so she asks him, "And where did you find it, dear?" So the boy says, "The maid has it now, and she's washing Daddy's face with it!"

****

Trailertrash Cletus was enjoying his normal Saturday afternoon activities (watching TV and drinking beer) when his wife came storming into the trailer. "Cletus, some man's been real rude to me and I want you to go and kick his ass!" she screamed. "Why, sure thing, Maylene," said Cletus, "you jus' tell me what he done did to you." "Well," said Maylene, "I was at the supermarket and I dropped something. When I bent over to pick it up this man looked up my dress." Cletus started stamping his feet. "And then, when I got back up, he said, 'I'd like to fill you up with beer and drink the lot from down there!'" Cletus sat down straight away. Maylene asked, "Ain't you goin' do nothin'," Cletus?' Cletus said, "You must be kidding, Maylene – I ain't gonna mess with someone who can drink that much beer!"

****

Two village idiots are discussing safe sex: "So, matey, how do you protect yourself from AIDS?" says the first. "I wear a condom constantly," says the second. "Don't you ever take it off?" says the first. "Of course: when I go to the bathroom and when I have sex!" says the second.

****

"So, Cletus; how did your first day of upper school go?" said Cletus' father. "It was great, Daddy," said Cletus. "Teacher asked each one of us to count to one hundred. Some of the kids couldn't get past the number 30, but I counted all the way to one hundred without making a single mistake. It was great." "That's great, son," said the father, "it's because you're from Arkansas." The next day the father asked, "So how was school today, Cletus?" Cletus said, "It was fine: we had to say the alphabet in class today, Daddy. Some of the kids couldn't get past the letter Q, but I got all the way from A to Z without any mistakes. It was great." 'That's great, son," said the father, "it's because you're from Arkansas." After the third day, Cletus came back with a worried look on his face. "What's the matter, son? No good news from school today?" asked Daddy. "Well, Daddy," said Cletus, "we had PE today, and after the lesson, in the shower, I noticed that I had the biggest weewee of anyone in the class. It must have been ten times longer and hairier than anyone else's. Is it because I'm from Arkansas?" "Not quite, son," said Daddy. "It's because you're 18 years old!'

****

Little Billy was famous for his rectal prowess, but it was starting to disrupt classes, so the teacher called him back after school to discuss the problem with him. She began by asking him why he kept breaking wind all the time when he knew it offended many people. "Well, miss, it's because I'm the best and I'm really proud of myself. I want to share my gift with the world." "So, in that case," said his teacher, "if I can do it better than you, will you stop doing it in the classroom?" Little Billy said he surely would, mainly because he didn't think she would be able to do it better than him. So the teacher set up the test: she placed two pieces of paper covered in chalk dust on the floor, the idea being to blow as much dust as possible from the paper. Little Billy steps forward first, drops his trousers and pants and crouches down over the paper. He rips out his best effort and it clears most of the chalk dust from the page. At the teacher's turn, she hitches up her skirt, drops her knickers and squats over her piece of paper. She lets fly a huge blast that completely clears the chalk dust and also blows the paper across the room. Little Billy is impressed and asks the teacher if she can repeat what she's just done. She is flattered, so agrees to do it just one more time. As she crouches down, Little Billy takes a quick peek up her skirt. "Hey, that's not fair," he begins. "No wonder you won, miss: yours is double-barrelled!"

✶✶✶✶

One upon a time a long way away there was a kingdom with a king who had a daughter. He wanted her to marry a brave man who would desire her and make her happy. So he devised a test: if any man could swim across his huge lake of crocodiles they could have the choice of a castle, untold riches or his daughter's hand in marriage. People gathered from miles around and many volunteered to try. "I can do it," a man cried, jumped into the water and was instantly swallowed up by the crocodiles. "I can do better than that," said another, who jumped in and was instantly swallowed up by the crocodiles. Next, there was a loud splash and a man began to swim. He made it all the way and was greeted by the king. "Would you like the castle, the cash or the fair princess, brave sir?" he asked. "None of them," the man replied, "I want the dirtag who pushed me in in the first place!"

****

A priest thinks his sermons need modernizing a bit, so he decides to preach on windsurfing instead of the usual fire and brimstone, or condemnation of sex. He tells his wife, who thinks it's a great idea, despite the priest's inexperience with the subject matter, but is sorry she won't be able to hear his new-style sermon because she has a sick friend to see. On his way to church the priest has second thoughts. "I don't know a thing about windsurfing and I can't relate it to anything," he said to himself. "I'll just stick to what I know," and proceeded to preach his usual sermon on the sinfulness of sex. After the service, and before the priest gets home, one of the lay readers walks past the priest's house. The priest's wife is back and out doing some gardening. "Great sermon today," says the lay reader. "That's a surprise," said the wife, "because he only tried it twice, and he fell off both times!"

****

A dull old maths teacher leaves a letter for his wife one Friday night:

Dear Janet,
As you know, I am 56, and by the time you read this letter I will be settled in at the Luxor Hotel, tucking into my beautiful, sexy, 21-year-old teaching assistant.

When the teacher arrives at the hotel he finds that a letter has been left for him:

Dear John,
As you know, I too am 56, and by the time you read this letter I will be settled in at the Excelsior Hotel, tucking into my handsome, virile, 21-year-old toyboy. You, being a maths teacher, will appreciate that 21 goes into 56 a lot more times than 56 goes into 21!

****

Mr Rennie was an old man and he lived in a nursing home. One day he walked into the nurses' quarters and told them his penis had died. None of them were shocked – this sort of thing happened all the time – and they just figured he was a bit bored and would get over it. A couple of days later, Mr Rennie bumped into one of the nurses walking down the corridor. His penis was hanging out of his trousers. The nurse said to him, "I thought your penis had died, Mr Rennie?" "It certainly did, young lady,' he replied, 'but today's the viewing!"

****

Four retired friends decide to go golfing. One of them pays the fees, while the other three go up to tee off. They are all bragging about their sons. The first man says, "Well, my son's in construction, and he's so successful that he gave one of his friends a brand-new house for free." The second man says, "Well, my son's a car salesman, and he's so successful that he gave one of his friends a Porsche for free." The third man says, "Well, my son's a stockbroker, and he's so successful that he gave one of his friends a share portfolio for free." At this point the fourth man arrives on the scene and they tell him, "We were just discussing how our sons were doing. Is yours successful?" The man says, "Well, my son is gay, and he's an erotic dancer in a gay bar." There is silence as the others look embarrassed for the man. "I'm not really thrilled about the dancing, but still," the man continues, "he does pretty well anyway. His last three boyfriends gave him a share portfolio, a Porsche and a brand-new house for nothing!"

✳✳✳✳

A German is climbing in the Alps when he stops for a rest. He notices a bottle half-hidden in the pile of stones that he is sitting on. He uncorks it and WHAM! a genie pops out. "Thank you for releasing me, O Great One," the genie says. "I can grant you one wish – it can be anything you want." The man has a think, and eventually says, "I'm a big fan of schnapps and it's rather expensive. Could you arrange for me to piss schnapps?" "Your wish is my command, O Great One," says the genie, who waves his hand and then disappears. The man carries on with his walk and eventually gets home. That evening, after dinner, he goes to the toilet. As he is going, he thinks to himself, "I wonder if that genie was telling the truth... let's see, now that smells like schnapps, and it looks like schnapps, so..." And he pees a bit into a glass. He holds it up to the light and then tastes just a tiny bit. "Hurrah! It is schnapps, and good schnapps at that," he shouts, and drinks the entire glass. The man rushes out of the bathroom calling for his wife, "Helga, Helga, come quickly: it's a miracle!" Helga comes downstairs and he "pours" her a glass of schnapps. She is very apprehensive and it is not until he drinks some himself that she will try the liquid. She finds the taste fantastic as well, so the two of them get blasted on top-quality schnapps all night and have a great time. The next day after work the German tells Helga to take two glasses out of the cupboard because they will be having another party. She willingly agrees and the couple party the night away on the excellent schnapps that the man "produces". The next day after work the German tells Helga to take only one glass out of the cupboard because they will be having another party. "But, my love," she says, "why only the one glass?" The man fills his glass, lifts it to his wife and says, "because tonight, my dear, you drink from the bottle!"

****

Three men, John, Jack and Jim, are shipwrecked and washed up on the shores of Africa. They turn inland looking for food and safety but are captured by cannibals. The cannibal king tells them that normally they eat everything they find in the forest, but that he will give them a chance to live if they pass a small test. The test is in two parts: for the first part, all they have to do is gather ten pieces of the same type of fruit in the forest. "Easy enough," the men think, and they all run off quickly. First of all John comes back with his arms full and walks up to the king of the cannibals. "I have brought apples, O cannibal king," he says. The cannibal king then explains the second part of the trial... "You will have the fruit forcibly inserted into your arsehole without any pain, pleasure or sentiment to be shown on your face. Any sentiment or sound whatever will cause you to be skinned alive and eaten." So John is bent over and the second part of the trial begins. The first apple goes in easily, but the second one is bigger and John winces as it is forced. As he cries out, he is carried away, prepared for the pot and eaten. Shortly Jack comes back with his hands full and walks up to the king of the cannibals. "I have brought blackberries, O cannibal king," he says. The cannibal king explains the second part of the trial and Jack grins to himself as he bends over. The insertion begins. First one berry, then two, then three, then four, then five, then six, then seven, then eight. Jack keeps his cool throughout, but suddenly, on the ninth berry, he bursts out laughing and is taken away, prepared for the pot and eaten. The two men meet up in Heaven. John says to Jack, "What happened to you then? I saw that you picked berries and I'd have thought you would have got through that with no problem." Jack says, "Me, too, and I was nearly there when I saw Jim coming round the corner with an armful of watermelons!"

****

Two cowboys are sat having a drink in a bar. One asks his friend if he's heard of the latest sexual position. Apparently it's called "the rodeo". The other says no and asks what you do. "Well," says the first cowboy, "first you mount your wife from the back, reach around her front and cup both breasts with your hands. Then you whisper softly in her ear, 'Oh baby, these are almost as nice as your sister's!' Then you see how long you can hang on for!"

****

Nikos, a Greek man, was sitting in a bar talking to a young tourist. "So," he says, "you see that wall out there in that field?" He points to a huge stone wall separating two fields. "Can you see how well it's built? I spent a year of my life moving stones from down in the valley up to those pastures and carving them so they fitted. That's the strongest fence between here and Athens! And do they call me Nikos the wall-builder? No; they do not!" Then he continues, "So, you see the bar here? The one you are leaning on right now?" and he raps it with his knuckles. 'Can you see how well it's built? I spent a year of my life cutting and sanding and waxing this bar. This is the finest bar between here and Athens! And do they call me Nikos the bar-builder? No, they do not!" Then he continues, "So, you see the pier out there in the water?" He points to a long, solid pier that stretches out into the deep, deep water. "I spent a year of my life putting that pier together. I cut down the trees, I nailed the boards and I dug the holes for the poles. It almost killed me, and it is the finest pier between here and Athens! And do they call me Nikos the pier-builder? No, they do not!" Then he looks around and checks the bar before he continues, "So I fuck *one* lousy sheep...!"

****

Jim and Nick are hanging out on the beach trying to pull. Nick has plenty of luck, but Jim's a bit short in the "front" so he says to Nick, "What's up, Nick? I'm just not having much luck with the ladies?" Nick replies, "It must be that you aren't appealing enough to the basic animal instincts. Try putting a nice big potato down your swimming trunks. The birds'll take one look and be all over you like a rash!" Now Jim knows that Nick pulls all over the place, so thinks he might as well give it a damn good go. The next day the two of them meet up again and Jim is in no better a mood. He says to Nick, "I tried it with that potato and you know, it did me no good at all. In fact, even more of the chicks are avoiding me than before. What's that all about?" Nick has a quick look and says, "Well, mate, I think it'd probably help a lot if you put the potato down the front!"

****

Two explorers are walking through a rainforest when they are captured by a tribe of tiny, but highly aggressive, cannibals. Minutes later they find themselves tied up tight, sitting in a huge pot full of water and vegetables with an enormous fire burning underneath it. After a couple of minutes one of them starts to laugh. The other one is shocked and assumes the man has lost his mind. "What the heck is up with you?" he asks, "We're going to die in here and be eaten by a bunch of horrible cannibals. What on earth do you find funny about that?" The other replies, "I just peed in the pot!"

****

A businessman goes on a trip to Japan. As is traditional, he and his associates all go out with their Japanese equivalents and get totally drunk. Then they send the American upstairs with a prostitute. As he begins to have sex with her, she starts to moan, "Nai com chai, nai com chai." He has no idea what it means, but she doesn't look very happy, so the businessman stops and leaves. The next day, he is out playing golf with his associates when one of his Japanese hosts slices the ball horribly to one side and in frustration shouts, "Nai com chai!" The American businessman says to him, "What does that mean?" The Japanese businessman replies, "Wrong hole!"

****

One night a guy had a few too many at his local and decided to drive home very slowly, taking the "clever" route to avoid any policemen or other snoopers. As he did so, he passed a field full of pumpkins. Having been drinking, the man was feeling pretty horny so started to think about how pumpkins are soft and squishy on the inside, and how no one need ever know, and how it wouldn't really do any harm, would it? So he pulled over and picked out a nice soft pumpkin, cut the right-sized hole in the side and began to have a go. He really started getting carried away and before he knew it he was sweating away, oblivious to the world: so oblivious, he didn't even notice a police car turn up right behind him. The two policemen walk up behind him and one of them shouts, "Hey sir, sir, do you realize you're fucking a pumpkin?" The man jumps, realizes he's been rumbled and starts thinking. Quick as a flash, he says, "A pumpkin? Is it midnight already, officer?"

****

Two mates are out for an evening in a bar. They happen to go to the toilet at the same time. As they are standing there, John notices that Thomas is pretty well-endowed and he can't help mentioning the fact. "Yeah," says Thomas. "But it wasn't always like that, you know. I was sick of only having a small one, so I had a transplant from a doctor in Harley Street. It was pretty expensive – £10,000 – but it was really worth it." A few months later, the two mates find themselves next to each other in a toilet again. John says to Thomas "I thought about what you said last time, and I decided to get myself a transplant, too. You got well ripped off, mate – mine only cost a grand!" Thomas leans across the urinals and has a quick look. "Not surprising," he says. "They've given you my old one!"

****

Two men are changing after a sweaty game of squash. One notices that the other has a cork up his arse. He says, "Um, I couldn't help noticing, but how the hell did you get that cork up your arse?" The other man says, "Well, um, yes: it's a bit embarrassing, really. I was walking along a beach barefoot when I trip over this old bottle. I pick it up, take the cork out and whoosh! Out pops a huge red man with a turban on his head, floating in space in front of me. He says 'I am a genie. I grant you one wish. What will it be?' So I – rather foolishly, upon reflection – said, 'No shit!'"

✱✱✱✱

A little old lady walks into a sex shop. She is having trouble walking and half hobbles and half hops over to the counter. She eventually makes it and holds on for dear life. She says the the boy behind the counter, "D-d-d-d-ooo yo-yo-you s-s-s-sell d-d-d-d-d-dildos-s-s-?" The boy says, "Yes, ma'am, we sell dildos. In fact we sell all sorts, in all shapes and sizes." The little old lady says, "D-d-d-d-d-o yo-yo-you h-h-h-h-have w-w-w-ww-wun th-th-th-th-that is sm-sm-sm-sm-small and b-b-b-b-black, s-s-s-s-s-ix i-i-i-i-i-inches l-l-l-l-ong b-b-b-b-b-but three i-i-i-i-i-inches th-th-th-th-thick?" The boy says, "Why, yes we do: that's one of the most popular models." "W-w-w-w-w-w-ell, c-c-c-c-c-c-can you t-t-t-t-t-t-tell m-m-m-me-e-e- how-w-w-w-w to t-t-t-t-t-turn-n-n-n-nn the fu-fu-fu-fucking thing-g-g-g-g-g- off-f-f-f-f-f-f-f-f-f-f?"

✱✱✱✱

173

Two men and a woman were sitting in a bar discussing their lives. The first man says, "You know, I'm a YUPpie – that's Young, Urban Professional." The second man says, "Well, me and my missus, we're DINKs – that's Double Income, No Kids." Then the first man asks the woman, "So what are you?" She replies, "I'm a WIFE – that's Wash, Iron, Fuck, Et cetera!"

****

There's this really vain surfer type. He jogs and he lifts weights and he stretches and he tones. He's admiring himself in the mirror one day and he notices that all of him looks great apart from his willy – it is the only part of him that doesn't have a tan. So he tries instant tan from all sorts of places and tanning booths, but nothing works. Eventually he goes to see a doctor who tells him that because of the sensitive nature of the skin, he will only be able to tan his willy in proper sunlight. So the man goes to the beach. Sadly, there are no nudist beaches near where he lives, so he goes to a normal one and tries to get himself a tan without anyone noticing. He can't manage it, so he develops a plan: he digs a hole big enough to hide in and buries himself, apart from his willy, which he leaves sticking out, and his mouth. He puts on suntan lotion and falls asleep. A few minutes later, a couple of little old ladies walk past and one of them notices the willy in the sand. She prods it a couple of times with her walking stick and gets it to wake up a little bit. Then she sighs and says to her friend, "There's no justice, is there?" "What do you mean, dear?" her friend replies. The lady says, "Well, I've spent my life being curious about willies, enjoying them, asking for them, tasting them, praying for more of them, hoping they'll get bigger, and now here I am, 80 years old – they grow wild on the beach and I can't even squat down!"

****

An accountant is thrown in prison for fraud and is seriously disappointed to see that his cellmate is a huge body-builder type with no hair and covered in tattoos. His new cellmate says, "Don't worry, number-boy, I'm in here for white collar crime as well." The accountant says, "Phew, that's lucky, I'm in for insider dealing and tax evasion. What about you?" The cellmate replies, "I murdered three priests!"

****

Superman is flying through the skies of the city feeling horny and looking for opportunities to score. Suddenly he sees Wonder Woman sunbathing naked on the top of a building. "Aw, she won't mind; and besides, I'll be so quick she'll hardly notice!" he says to himself. He swiftly flies down, fucks her in quadruple-quick time and shoots off. Wonder Woman jumps up and says, "What the hell was that?" to which the Invisible Man replies, "I don't know, but my bum sure hurts!"

****

Three young female students all lived together in a flat and one night they all had dates at the same time. Around midnight they all got back and started comparing notes. The first girl says, "You know what? You can tell a good date when you come back home and your hair's all messed up." And the second girl says, "You know what? You can tell a good date when you come back home and your make-up's all smeared." The third girl says nothing, but just reaches under her skirt, removes her knickers and throws them against the wall. They stick there. "You know what? That's a good date," she says.

****

A mounted policeman was on patrol one day when he comes across a little boy on a shiny new bicycle. The policeman leans down to the boy and says, "That's a nice shiny bike. Did Father Christmas bring it for you?" "He sure did," says the boy, all pleased with himself. Then the cop sits back up and writes the boy a £25 fine. "Next year, boy," he says, "ask Father Christmas to put a licence plate on it, too." The boy is really annoyed, so decides to get his own back. He looks up at the policeman and says, "That's a fine horse. Did Father Christmas bring it for you?" The policeman, thinking he will humour the boy, says, "He sure did," and is pretty pleased with himself. The boy then looks down underneath the horse and back up at the policeman before saying, "Next year, officer, perhaps you could ask Father Christmas to put the prick underneath the horse instead of on top!"

****

Two village idiots go to a brothel and hammer on the door. "What the hell do you want?" shouts the madam."We've come for women," say the idiots. "How much money do you have on you?" shouts the madam again. The idiots scrabble through their pockets and see. "We've got a tenner!" they shout. "For that much you can go screw yourselves," laughs the madam. Just five minutes later, the idiots return and bang on the door again: "We've screwed ourselves: now we've come to give you the tenner!" they shout.

****

A couple had children who were very inquisitive, so were finding it hard to communicate about "adult" things like having sex. To avoid having to teach the children about the birds and the bees, they decide to use a code instead, using the word "typewriter" as a substitute for sex. A couple of days later the husband thinks it will be amusing to use the code for the first time, so he calls his five-year-old daughter over and says to her, "Go and tell your mother that Daddy would like her to come up and type a letter on the typewriter, please." The girl goes off and comes back a couple of minutes later. She says, "Mummy says that she can't type a letter for Daddy today because she's got a red ribbon stuck in the typewriter." A few days later the daughter comes up to the father and says, "Mummy told me to tell you that she can type that letter now." The father says, "Well, you go and tell Mummy not to worry because Daddy couldn't wait for the typewriter, so he decided to write the letter by hand!"

****

Once upon a time there was a sweet little girl who always wore pretty little dresses to school. However, at lunchtime every day she would sit on the bench by the tuckshop and cry. Nobody knew why, so one day one of her classmates, Tony, plucked up the courage to ask her why she always cried. She explained that she really loved chocolate but that she never had any money to buy some. So Tony says to her, "Tell you what: if you climb up that tree over there, I'll give you the money to buy some chocolate." "That's just great," the little girl says, and she runs off to climb the tree. As she does so, Tony and all the other boys in her class gather round and watch her climb. As she gets down, Tony gives her the money and thanks her. The next day the same thing happens and the sweet little girl climbs the tree again to get the chocolate. Again, all the boys watch her go up and down. This becomes a daily occurence at school and eventually the girl's mother asks her where she gets her chocolate money from. "It's easy, mum," the sweet little girl explains. "The boys in my class all give me money to climb the tree every day." "Oh, dear, don't do that: those nasty boys just want to see your underwear as you climb." "OK, mum," the girl says; but the next day at lunchtime there is an even bigger crowd by the tree as the sweet little girl climbs it. When she gets home that evening her mother asks her where she got her chocolate that day. "Oh, mum: I got it from climbing the tree," she explains simply, but the mother says, "Honey, I told you not to do that. Those boys just want to see your underwear!" So the sweet little girl says, "Don't worry, mum: I didn't wear any underwear today!"

****

An Italian, a Frenchman and an Irishman are all chatting about their love-making prowess. The Italian begins by saying, "When I have feeneesh make-a love with my-a wife, I just stroke her-a buttocks and she-a float seex eenches above-a tha bed in total ecstasy." The Frenchman continues, "Zat's noseeng. When I av-a feeneeshed to make ze lurve wiz my wife, I leek ze solez of 'er feet and she float 12 eenches above ze bed in total ecstasy!" So the Irishman says, "Well, when I've screwed da woife, I git out da bed, wipe me dick on da curtins and she hits da fukkin' roof!"

****

A decent young man goes for dinner at his new girlfriend's house. He is very anxious and keen to impress his prospective in-laws. As the meal is served the family dog comes out of its basket, sits on the floor right beside the dinner table and proceeds to start licking its balls with a massively loud slurping sound. There is a shocked silence: nobody knows where to look or what to say. Driven to a state of wild nervousness, the man stutters, "Um, er, um... I er wish I could do that!" The girlfriend's family all look around in even greater shock and the mother says to him, "Well, if you gave him a biscuit I'm sure he'd let you!"

****

Three soldiers come back from active duty in Afghanistan. They are all due for retirement and are all summoned before their commanding officer. He tells them that in addition to their Army pension they will be paid a premium for services rendered in the Middle East and it will be calculated in the following way: each man will be paid $100 for a measurement from two points in their body, the two points to be stipulated by the men themselves. So the first soldier, a Sergeant, walks up to the front. "Where do you want the measurements to be taken from, Sergeant?" says the CO. "From the top of my shaved head to the tip of my toes, Sir!" A Lieutenant makes the measurement and tells the Commanding Officer it is 71 inches. "Seventy-one inches!" says the Commanding Officer. "That makes $7,100 for you." So the second soldier, a Corporal, walks up to the front. "Where do you want the measurements to be taken from, Corporal?" says the Commanding Officer. "From my left fingertip to my right fingertip, Sir!" says the Corporal. A Lieutenant makes the measurement and tells the CO it is 73 inches. "Seventy-three inches!" says the Commanding Officer, "that makes $7,300 for you." So the third soldier, a Private, walks up to the front. "Where do you want the measurements to be taken from, Private?" says the Commanding Officer. "From the top of my penis to the base of my balls, Sir!" says the Private. The commanding officer is a little surprised, but gets the lieutenant to make the measurement anyway. After a couple of seconds the Lieutenant says from down below, "Where on earth are your balls, Private?" and the private replies, "Back in Osama Bin Laden's bunker, Sir!"

****

An ambassador from an African country was visiting Russia. The Russian ambassador to his country was entertaining him, and despite the obvious cultural differences, the two of them got on really well. The African gentleman was impressed by the hospitality that he was shown and on the final day of the visit the Russian offered to show him the traditional game of the country – Russian Roulette. The African man had not heard of this game, so the Russian explained the rules. "You pick up a revolver. You empty the cylinder. You replace one bullet. You spin the cylinder. You turn the gun to yourself and pull the trigger once." The African ambassador found this a bit scary, but coming from a proud warrior people he thought it would be exciting. The Russian man produced two revolvers and when both guns were loaded, both men turned them on themselves and pulled the triggers at the same time. There were two loud clicks and both breathed a huge sigh of relief. The African ambassador was very impressed with the game and thought about it all the way home. One year later, the Russian ambassador visited the Africa country to finalize a deal between the two countries. His hospitality was returned, much to his pleasure, and he and the African ambassador got on as well as before. On his last night, the African man said he would show him his country's traditional game. The Russian was impressed, and eager to see what the African had to offer him. The African ambassador led him to a plush room, deep in the state building. Standing before them were six beautiful women, all completely naked. The African said,

"These are the most beautiful women from each of the six tribes of the country. Any one of them will give you the best blowjob of your life – just choose one." The Russian was impressed, but he couldn't help feeling there was something missing from this "game". He said to the African ambassador, "That's great and everything, but compared to the national game from my country there is something missing – where's the danger, the excitement, the chance?" The African ambassador, with a wide grin on his face, answers, "One of these women is a cannibal!"

****

There were twin brothers by the name of Joey and John Jones. They had lived in the same fishing village all their lives. John was married and Joey had always been single. Joey owned a knackered old boat. One day, Joey's boat sank on exactly the same day that John's wife passed away. A couple of days later a kindly old lady met Joey in the queue for the Post Office and she thought he was John. She said to him, "So sorry for your trouble: you must be feeling awful and I'm not surprised." Joey, not at all worried about his crappy old boat, replied, "Well, I couldn't care less. She was a pile of crap right from the very beginning. Her bottom was all lumpy and she always stank of old fish. The first time I got in her she leaked faster than anything I'd ever seen before in my life. She had a crack and a huge hole in front that kept getting bigger and bigger every time that I used her. I could handle her fine, but when someone else was using her she leaked like a bastard and that's what finished her off, I reckon: three or four blokes from out of town came over looking for a good time. I told them that she was useless and much too creaky for all of them, but they really thought she looked all right. Anyway, all of them tried to get into her at the same time. It was just too much and she cracked right up the middle!" The little old lady fainted!

✸✸✸✸

On a sunny, hot afternoon a man is sitting on his porch drinking iced lemonade in a deckchair relaxing and watching as his wife grunts, groans and struggles with the lawnmower. The next-door neighbour can't believe her eyes and she storms over to the porch. "You should be ashamed of yourself, you caveman, letting your wife mow the lawn on a day like this. You ought to be hung!" "I am," says the man with a wry smile, "and that's exactly why my wife is mowing the lawn."

✸✸✸✸

One morning at breakfast, Chuck walks up behind his wife and pinches her arse. "You know, Daisy, if you firmed this up we'd be able to get rid of your girdle," he says. Now Daisy is most insulted by this, of course, but she decides to let it go – it's only breakfast time, after all. The next day, Chuck walks up behind his wife and pinches her breast. "You know, Daisy, if you firmed this up we'd be able to get rid of your bra," he says. Daisy can't bite her lip another time, so she turns around and grasps his cock firmly, saying, "You know, Chuck, if you firmed this up we'd be able to get rid of the postman, the gardener, the pool man and your brother!"

****

Blonde

Ambition

Not for the
fair-haired

A blonde is walking down the street with a pig under her arm. She passes a man who, puzzled, asks "Where did you get that?" "I won her in a raffle!" the pig replies.

****

One day, a blonde went to see the doctor with a carrot in one ear, a cucumber in the other and two peas up her nose, complaining she wasn't feeling well. The doctor told her it was because she wasn't eating properly.

****

Three blondes witness a violent crime. Two days later, they are summoned by the police to identify a suspect. In order to check they are reliable witnesses, the inspector says he will show them a mug-shot for 30 seconds, then ask each one for a description. He shows the mug-shot to the first blonde for 30 seconds, then covers it and asks her if she thinks she would recognize the face. "Yes, easy," she replies. "The guy in the picture has only one eye." The inspector blinks in confusion, then says, "He's got only one eye because it's a profile shot!" Shaking his head, he repeats the procedure for the second blonde and again asks if she would recognize him. "Easy! He only has one ear," she answers. "Come on, what's the matter with you two? It's a profile shot! You're seeing this man from the side!" shouts the inspector. Expecting the worst, he repeats the procedure with the third blonde, then says, 'Would you recognize the suspect from this picture if you saw him in real life? And think before you give me a stupid answer." The third blonde looks hard at the photo, and remains silent for a minute, then says, "Yeah, it's easy: he's wearing contact lenses." This takes the inspector by surprise. He picks up the photo and looks really hard at it, but can't tell if the suspect wears contact lenses or not. With a suspicious look at the third blonde, he checks the full report on the suspect. Sure enough, when the mug-shot was taken, he was wearing contact lenses! Baffled, the inspector goes back to the third blonde and asks her, "How could you tell he was wearing contact lenses?" "Well," she says, "he can't wear regular glasses with only one eye and one ear, now, can he?"

****

Two blondes are waiting at the bus stop. A bus pulls up and the doors open. The first blonde steps in and asks the driver: "Will this bus take me to New Street?" "Sorry, it won't: you're at the wrong stop," the driver replies. The second blonde steps inside, throws her chest out, smiles devilishly and twitters: "Will it take ME?"

****

A blonde walks into a library and says to the librarian at the counter, "Can I have a burger and fries, please?" "This is a library," the librarian answers reprovingly. "Oh, I'm so sorry. *May* I have a burger and fries?" the blonde whispers.

****

A blonde is complaining to her friend about her boyfriend and men in general. "I've had enough with men. They're cheap, they cheat on you, they don't respect you... Next time I want sex, I'll use my trusty plastic companion instead." "Yeah, but what will you do when the batteries run out?" her friend asks. "I'll fake an orgasm as usual."

****

A guy approaches the window of the ticket office of a cinema carrying a chicken in his arms. "Hi: could I get two tickets, please? Oh – does my pet chicken have to pay full price?" "What do you mean, your pet chicken? Chickens aren't allowed into the cinema," the girl tells him. Outraged, he storms off, but after a few minutes, as he really wants to see this film, he decides to hide his chicken in his pants and try again. He returns to the booth and this time, to his delight, he is allowed to get a ticket. During the film, however, he can feel the chicken getting restless so he pulls his zip down and lets its head out for some fresh air. As it happens, he's sitting next to two blondes. One of them, turning to check what he's doing wiggling in his seat, turns to her friend and says: "Sally, the guy sitting next to me just unzipped his flies!" "It's OK; when you've seen one, you've seen them all," the other replies. "Yes, but this one is eating my popcorn!"

****

A blonde is looking at a bulletin board at her workplace and sees an ad which says, "Luxury Ocean Cruise Only €5." She copies the details, goes to the address and hands the ad and a fiver to the secretary. The secretary points to a burly guy sitting in a battered sofa, reading a newspaper. The guy stands up and knocks the blonde unconscious. When she wakes up, she's tied to a log and floating down the river. She starts to think maybe this wasn't such a good idea after all. Then she sees one of her colleagues (who is also blonde) floating right next to her. Sighing, she says, "So do you think they're going to serve us some food on this trip?" "They didn't last year," the other blonde replies.

****

A mother and her young blonde daughter have just finished shopping for food and all the groceries are scattered over the kitchen floor in plastic bags. While the mum busies herself putting things away, the daughter picks up a box of animal crackers and empties its contents on the table, making quite a mess. "What are you doing?" her mum yells. "Well, it says on the box, 'Do not eat if seal is broken.' I'm looking for the seal."

****

How do you know a blonde has been sending e-mail?
There's an envelope in the CD drive.

How do you know a blonde is having a bad day?
Her tampon's behind her ear and she can't find her cigarette.

How do you get a twinkle in a blonde's eye?
Shine a flashlight in her ear.

How do blondes' brain cells die?
Alone.

Did you hear about the new blonde paint?
It's not real bright, but it's cheap and it spreads easy.

How do you know that a blonde's been using a word processor?
There's Tippex all over the screen.

What's a blonde's favourite nursery rhyme?
Humpme Dumpme.

What do blondes and doorknobs have in common?

Everyone gets a turn.

****

A blonde wanted to get her pet dog in a smooth-haired dog contest and decided to help her dog a little by going to the chemist for some hair-removal lotion. The assistant hands her a bottle of special shampoo and says: "Remember to keep your arms in the air for at least three minutes." "Er, it's not for my armpits," the blonde replies blushing slightly, "it's for my Chihuahua." "In that case, don't ride a bike for three days," the assistant says.

****

A blonde is flying on a four-engined plane. Suddenly there's a loud bang, the pilot comes on the radio and says, "I'm sorry, but we seem to have lost an engine. We'll probably be delayed by 45 minutes." A few minutes later, there's another bang. Once again, the radio comes on: "I'm sorry, but we seem to have lost another engine. We'll probably be delayed by two hours." A little while later, the third engine shuts off. This time, the pilot tells the passengers that they will be delayed by around three hours. The blonde turns to the guy sitting beside her and says, "Man, if they lose the fourth engine, we'll be up here all day."

****

A blonde is taking a tour of a National Park and hears the guide say dinosaur fossils have been found in the area. "Wow!" she exclaims. "I'd never have thought dinosaurs would come so close to the motorway."

****

NASA sends a space shuttle up with two pigs and a blonde on board. While the shuttle is taking off, the NASA command centre calls the first pig and asks, "Pig One, do you know your mission?" The pig replies, "Oink oink. Get the shuttle into orbit and launch the trillion-dollar satellite. Oink oink." Then Mission Control asks the second pig, "Pig Two, do you know your mission?" The second pig replies, "Oink oink. Once Pig One has completed the trillion-dollar satellite launch, close hatch and land shuttle. Oink oink." Then NASA asks the blonde, "Blonde woman, do you know your mission?" The blonde woman replies, "Um... Oh yeah: I remember now. Feed the pigs – and *Don't touch a goddamned thing!*"

****

A blonde walks down the street and sees a banana peel on the ground 100 metres ahead. "Here we go again," she sighs.

****

A blonde goes to the electrical appliance sale and finds a bargain. She stops a salesman and says: "I'd like to buy this TV, please." "Sorry: we don't sell to blondes," the salesman replies. She storms out of the shop and hurries home, where she dyes her hair. She comes back to the same shop and again tells the salesman: "I'd like to buy this TV, please." "Sorry: we don't sell to blondes," he replies again. "How did he recognize me?" she wonders. Mortified, she rushes back home again and goes for the complete disguise this time – haircut, new colour, new outfit, big sunglasses – then waits a full day before returning to the shop. "I'd like to buy this TV, please," she says to the same man. "Sorry: we don't sell to blondes," he replies. Frustrated, she exclaims, "But how do you know I'm a blonde?" "Because that's not a TV: it's a microwave," he replies.

****

"The guys down at the pub say the milkman has seduced every woman on our street except one," Bob told his blonde wife. She thought for a moment. "I'll bet it's that snooty Mrs. Jenkins."

****

A blonde went to the hospital emergency room with the tip of her left index finger blown off. "How did this happen?" the doctor asked. "Well you see, I was trying to commit suicide," the blonde replied. "By shooting your finger?" the doctor asked, baffled. "No, silly! First I put the gun to my chest and I thought, 'I just paid \$6,000 for these boobs: no way I am blowing them off.' Then I put the gun in my mouth but I thought, 'I just paid $2,000 to get my teeth fixed: the teeth are staying!' So I put the gun in my ear and I thought, 'This is going to make a loud noise,' so I put my finger in my other ear before I pulled the trigger."

****

A blonde, a brunette and a redhead are running away from the cops when they stumble by chance upon an old barn to hide in. They find three big sacks on the floor of the barn and promptly jump in them. About a minute later, a police car comes to a screaming halt by the barn door and a policeman steps out. He enters the barn and spots the suspicious-looking sacks. He kicks the first one. "Meow," says the redhead. "It must be a cat," says the policeman, and he kicks the second sack. "Woof," says the brunette. "Must be a dog," mutters the policeman, and he kicks the third sack. "Potatoes," says the blonde.

****

A blonde finds her way to her doctor and tells him that she's really worried because every part of her body hurts. "Show me where," says the doctor, concerned. The blonde touches her own arm and screams, "Ouch!" Next she touches her leg, her nose, her elbow and every time she howls in pain. She looks at her doctor and says, "See? I told you: it hurts everywhere!" The doctor pokes her in the chest and says, "Don't worry; it's not serious. You've just got a broken index finger."

****

It is winter and a blonde decides to go ice-fishing. After having spent some time getting all the right tools, she drives toward the nearest frozen lake and starts cutting a circular hole in the ice. Then from the heavens a voice boomed, *"There are no fish under the ice."* Startled, the blonde moves a bit further down the ice, pours herself a mug of coffee from a thermos and starts cutting another hole in the ice. Out of nowhere, the voice booms, *"There are no fish under the ice."* This time the blonde is pretty scared, so she moves to the far end of the frozen lake. Just as she starts cutting another hole, the very loud voice says, *"There are no fish under the ice."* The awed, and very scared, blonde slowly raises her head and says, in a small, contrite voice: "Is that you, Lord?" The voice answers, "No. It is the manager of the ice rink!"

****

A blonde orders a pizza. When it is done, the cook asks her: "Do you want me to cut it into six or 12 pieces?" "Six, please," she says, "I couldn't eat 12 pieces."

****

A blonde and a brunette are out driving. As they've had a few beers, the brunette tells the blonde to look out for cops. They drive for a while, and then the blonde taps the brunette on the shoulder and says: "Hold on, there's a cop car behind us." "Shit!" says the brunette. "Are their lights on?" The blonde has to think for a moment, then says, "Er... Yes. No. Yes. No. Yes. No..."

****

Two American tourists were travelling through Wales. As they approached Llangollen, they started arguing about the pronunciation of the town's name until they stopped for lunch. As they stood at the counter, one tourist asked the blonde employee, "Could you settle an argument for us? Would you please pronounce where we are very slowly?" The blonde leaned over and said, "Burrrrrrr Gurrrrrr Kingggg."

****

A blonde, a redhead and a brunette were looking at a dictionary for the hardest words they knew. The brunette's word was "posthumous". The redhead's word was "deoxyribonucleic". The blonde's word was "dick".

****

A blonde, a brunette and a redhead are having a breaststroke swimming competition across the English Channel. The brunette finishes first, then the redhead second, but the blonde never finished. When the lifeboat found her, way behind, she said, "I don't want to be a telltale or anything, but the other two – you know? They used their arms."

****

A blonde was having a great time at a party and was soon spotted by a guy who swiftly led her upstairs. He started to undress her, then, surprised, saw that she was wearing shower caps on her tits. "Hey, what's with the shower caps?" the guy asked her. "What shower caps?" she answered, "These are booby condoms!"

****

A blonde, a brunette and a redhead go trekking one day and stumble upon a cave, in which there is an old magical mirror. The dusty book next to it says that this mirror will grant a wish only if you tell the truth – if you lie, you disappear in a puff of smoke. They find this pretty neat, so the brunette goes first. "I think I'm the smartest woman on earth." "Poof!" She disappears. The redhead goes up to try. "I think I'm the prettiest woman on earth." "Poof!" She disappears. The blonde goes up, decided to tell the truth and nothing but the truth. "I think…" "Poof!"

****

A little boy is playing with his blonde friend when another, older boy comes in. "I found a condom on the veranda," he smirks. The blonde looks up and asks innocently: "What's a veranda?"

****

After watching a program about Egyptians on TV, a blonde decides to treat herself to a milk bath. She leaves a note to the milkman which reads, "30 litres of milk tomorrow, please." On finding the note in the morning, the milkman is a bit confused and knocks on the door. "You mean three litres, right?" "No, you read right, 30 litres, please," the blonde smiles back. "Er...OK. Pasteurized?" "No: just up to my tits."

****

A blonde, a brunette and a redhead are on a walk in the mountains when they find a bridge over a deep ridge. They are halfway across when a fairy appears out of nowhere. "Welcome to the fairy bridge," she says. "If you want to pass, you need to jump over and shout the name of an animal: then you will be transformed into this animal and land harmlessly." The brunette goes first and, as she jumps over the edge of the bridge, she shouts "Lion!" and, sure enough, whoosh! she gets transformed into a great lion which gently descends to the ground and disappears into the trees. When it is her turn, the redhead swings her legs over the edge of the bridge and shouts "Eagle!" and whoosh! she is transformed into a magnificent eagle which soars to the heavens. The blonde finds this pretty neat but, just as she jumps over the bridge, she realizes she hasn't thought about what animal she wanted to be. "Crap," she says.

****

A young blonde was on vacation in the depths of Louisiana. She had always wanted a pair of genuine alligator shoes and thought it was the perfect place to get some. She was disappointed, however, for the local shoe shops were still too expensive for her. Very frustrated, she decided to catch her own alligator so that she could get a pair of shoes at a reasonable price. Later in the day a man was driving home after a day of fly-fishing when he spotted the blonde standing waist-deep in the water, shotgun in hand. Just then, horrified, he saw a huge nine-foot alligator swimming quickly toward her. The blonde took aim, squeezed the trigger and killed the beast. She waded to the body and dragged it to the bank, where there were already half a dozen dead alligators lying in the mud. With an angry shout, the blonde flipped the alligator on its back, stared at it for a few seconds and howled out, "Damn it: this one isn't wearing any shoes either!"

****

A blonde was trying to put together a jigsaw puzzle. She got very frustrated, so she decided to ask her husband for help. "It's supposed to be a tiger!" she cried. "Honey," said her husband, "put the Frosties back in the box!"

****

A blonde and a brunette are sitting in a pub having a drink when the brunette's boyfriend comes in with a bunch of roses. The brunette receives the flowers with apparent pleasure, but makes a face as soon as her boyfriend is off to get a drink from the bar. "Crap: he's bought me flowers again," says the brunette. "What's the matter with you? You don't like flowers?" asks her friend. "Oh, I do," the brunette replies. "It's just that when he buys me flowers it means I'll have to spend the next two or three days with my legs wide open." The blonde asks, "You don't have a vase?"

****

A blonde has been asked on a date and is being treated to a seafood restaurant. On her way to her table, they pass an aquarium full of live lobsters. At the end of the meal, taking pity on the lobsters, she manages to get near the aquarium while her date is settling the bill and hides a couple of them in her bag. "Neat," she thinks triumphantly. "I'll ask Bill to stop by the woods and I'll free the poor creatures."

****

Two blondes take a stroll in the forest. Suddenly, one blonde stops and looks down. "Look at those deer tracks," she says to her friend. Her friend looks down and replies: "These aren't deer tracks: they're wolf tracks." "No way. They're deer tracks." "You're completely wrong. These are *wolf* tracks!" They kept on arguing for half an hour, at which point they got killed by a train.

****

A blonde walks into a clothing store. She looks around for a while and finally picks out a scarf and brings it to the counter to pay for it. As she seems very pleased with her purchase, the cashier is surprised to see her again a hour or so later, holding the scarf out for a refund. "But this colour goes so well with your hair," the shop assistant remarks. "Why do you want to return it?" "Because it's too tight!" the blonde replies.

****

A blonde, a brunette and a redhead have been stuck on a deserted island for a long, long time when one day a magic lamp is washed ashore. The redhead rubs it hard and out pops a genie. "Thank you for letting me out of this bottle," he says. "As a reward, I can give a wish to each of you." The redhead goes first: "I hate it here. It is too hot and boring. I want to go home!" "All right," replied the genie, and the redhead disappears in a puff of smoke. Then it's the brunette's turn. "I miss my family, my friends and relatives. I want to go home, too!" "No sweat," the genie says and off she goes. Then the blonde starts crying and says, "I'm lonely: I wish my two friends were back here with me!"

****

A butcher is introducing his blonde wife: "Hello, everyone," he says. "Meet Patti."

****

A nervous blonde goes to the dentist. To calm her down, the dentist decides to tell her a short story. He thinks for a while, while putting his latex gloves on, then he has it. "Do you know how they make these gloves?" he asks genially to his patient. "There's a factory in Wales where there's a big vat of latex. They employ people of all ages, with various hand sizes, to dip their hands in the vat. They walk for a while until the latex solidifies a bit, then they take the gloves off." This story seems to have done the trick, because the blonde is smiling, a dreamy expression on her face. "I wonder where they make condoms," she breathes.

****

A blonde is arrested at the airport check-in for having a bomb in her bag and is being grilled by the customs officer: "How come you have a bomb in your bag?" he barks. "It's just because I'm afraid of flying," the blonde wails. "You are afraid of flying, therefore you carry a bomb with you?" "Oh, I'm just afraid someone will bring a bomb on the plane." The customs officer shakes his head to try and clear his thoughts and asks again, in an incredulous tone: "If you're afraid of someone carrying a bomb with them on a plane, why do *you* carry one?" "It's simple," replies the blonde. "I figured the odds against two people carrying a bomb with them would be much higher, so the plane would be far safer."

****

Blondes know that coughing can have bad consequences. Especially coughing in the wardrobe.

****

There is no such thing as an impotent man – only incompetent blondes.

****

A blonde finds herself, inexplicably, in a university and meets a professor of psychology. Not wanting to appear as if she didn't belong here, she asks him: "Tell me, Professor, is it true there's a way to detect mental deficiency in people that appear completely normal?" "Oh, yes," the professor answers. "All you have to do is ask them a very simple question which anybody can answer, and then monitor their replies." "Really? Have you got an example?" the blonde asks, vaguely planning on fooling the professor next time she meets him. "Take this one: Captain Cook did three trips to the Pole and died during one of them. Which one was it?" The blonde laughs nervously and said: "Can you give me another example? I'm not very good at history."

****

A blonde walks up to the counter of the local library and complains to the librarian: "Here's your book back. It's the most boring book I have ever read. There's no plot whatsoever, and far too many characters." "Oh, thank you," the librarian replies. "You must be the person who borrowed our phone book."

****

A blonde has been in a taxi for some time when she realizes she doesn't have any money. "I'm sorry," she says to the driver, "you'll have to go back, I forgot my purse and it is already £10." The driver glances at her and says: "It's OK: I'll just stop in a dark alley and you can take off your bra." "I can't do that: you'd be cheating yourself," the blonde replies. "Cheating myself? How so?" "This bra only cost me a fiver."

****

A young man stops at an ice cream van and asks the blonde serving: "What flavours do you have?" "Vanilla, chocolate, strawberry…" then she sneezes violently and her throat makes a rasping voice. "Have you got laryngitis?" he enquires in a sympathetic voice. "No, only vanilla, chocolate and strawberry."

****

It is a beautiful day and a young blonde and her boyfriend are visiting the zoo. The blonde is dressed in a tight-fitting dress which shows quite a bit of shapely leg and boob – and there's plenty of it to show! They arrive in front of the gorillas' cage and it is obvious that her dress is impressing the male gorilla, as he starts jumping up and down staring at her. "It looks like he fancies you," the boyfriend says. He suggests she plays a game on the poor beast and she purses her lips, wiggles her bottom and plays along for a while. The gorilla is getting wild with excitement, pounding his chest and grunting, to the amusement of the blonde and her boyfriend. At this point, the said boyfriend suggests she "accidentally" drops one of the flimsy straps of her dress. The blonde does that and this sends the gorilla into such a sexual frenzy that he seizes the bars of the cage, pulls them apart, grabs the girl and drags her into the cage with him, squeezing the bars back into place after him and glaring at the boyfriend who says, a triumphant note in his voice: "Now, you tell *him* you have a headache!"

****

A young ventriloquist is touring the clubs and one night does a show in a pub in Shropshire. With his puppet on his knee, he's going through his usual dumb blonde routine when a blonde woman stands on her chair and starts shouting angrily: "I've heard enough of your stupid blonde jokes. What makes you think you can stereotype women that way? What does the colour of a person's hair have to do with her worth as a human being? It's guys like you who keep women like me from being respected at work and in the community and from reaching our full potential, because you and your kind continue to perpetuate discrimination against not only blondes, but women in general!" The ventriloquist, embarrassed, begins to apologize, but the blonde yells, "You stay out of this, buster! I'm talking to that little jerk on your knee!"

****

A blonde is sitting at the counter in a bar with a glass of vodka with an olive in it. She tries to pick the olive up with the toothpick but it always eludes her, skidding to the other end of the glass. This futile exercise has been going on for half an hour when the man next to her, exasperated, snatches the toothpick from her hand and adroitly skewers the olive in one stroke. "This is how you do it," he says to the blonde. "Big deal," the blonde mutters darkly. "I already had him so tired out, he couldn't get away."

****

Three blondes go to a funfair and buy a raffle ticket. As it is for charity, everyone wins a small prize. The first blonde wins a case of spaghetti sauce. The second wins a small Stilton cheese. The third wins a toilet brush. The following day, they meet at the first blonde's place and she says: "Wasn't that great? I love spaghetti!" "And I adore cheese," comments the second blonde, then asks the third: "How's the toilet brush?" "Not so good , I'm afraid," she answers. "In fact, I think I'll go back to paper."

****

How do you give a blonde a maths class?
Subtract her clothes, divide her legs and give her a square root.

Why couldn't the blonde add ten and seven on a pocket calculator?
She couldn't find the ten key.

What's the difference between a smart blonde and the Abominable Snowman?
Maybe someday we'll find the Abominable Snowman.

What do you call a blonde with two brain cells?
Pregnant.

Why don't blondes take birth control pills?
Because they keep falling out.

What do blondes and shrimps have in common?
Their heads are full of shit, but the pink bits are nice.

What's the connection between a blonde and a halogen headlamp?
They both get screwed on the front of a Ford Escort.

What are a blonde's first words after two years of university?
"Would you like some ketchup?"

How do you give a blonde a brain transplant?
You blow in her ear.

How can you tell when a blonde rejects a new brain transplant?
She sneezes.

Why does "TGIF" on blondes' T-shirts stand for?
"Tits Go In Front."

How can you tell a blonde has been playing a game on the computer?
The joystick is wet.

What do you call a blonde who can't swim?
Shark bait!

What's the advantage of having a blonde as a girlfriend?
You get to park in handicapped zones.

To a blonde, what is long and hard?
Primary school.

What do a blonde and a car have in common?
They can both drive you crazy.

What did the blonde say when she saw a herd of elephants walking across the plains with sunglasses on?
Nothing: she didn't recognize them.

How many blondes does it take to change a light bulb?
One hundred: one to hold the light bulb, the other 99 to rotate the house.

What do a blonde and a taxi have in common?
Everyone's been in and out for a fiver.

What does a blonde use for protection during sex?
A bus shelter.

What do a blonde and a turtle have in common?
They're both screwed on their backs.

What does a blonde say after having multiple orgasms?
"Great work, team!"

What is it called when a blonde blows in another blonde's ear?
Data transfer.

How do you change a blonde's mind?
You buy her another beer.

What do you call a blonde with a runny nose?
Full.

What do a blonde and a beer bottle have in common?
They're both empty from the neck up.

Why do blonde mums only change their babies' nappies every month?
Because the instructions say, "Good for up to 20 pounds."

What do you say to a blonde with no arms and no legs?
Nice tits!

How do you play Space Invaders with a blonde?
You trap a fly in her head.

What did the little blonde girl say to her dad when she opened the box of Cheerios?
"Look, daddy: doughnut seeds!"

What do you call five blondes at the bottom of a swimming pool?
Air pockets.

What do you call a blonde in a university?
A visitor.

Why did God create blondes?
Because sheep can't bring beer from the fridge.

Why don't blondes like to breast-feed their babies?
It hurts too much to boil their nipples.

What do you call a pimple on a blonde's bum?
A brain tumour.

****

A blonde wanted to buy a personalized license plate for her new car but she couldn't afford it. So, instead, she decided to change her name to K34GML.

****

A blonde was strolling down the avenue when she saw a student wearing a sandwich board saying "Free Big Mac". She went up to him and asked: "Why? What did he do?"

****

A blonde, a brunette and a redhead go out sailing, but a storm damages their craft and they end up being blown onto a beautiful but uninhabited island. After a couple of days, they reach the conclusion that their absence has not been noticed. The redhead says, "Listen girls, we are trapped on this island; we have enough food for about two more days, but it can't be more than six or seven kilometres to the mainland and I am sure I can swim there." With that she dives into the water. She is quite a strong swimmer and she thinks she is making good headway. Sadly, the wind is blowing off the mainland and she has actually gone less than halfway when she begins to get very tired. She tries to go on, but exhaustion takes over and she drowns. A day later, when nothing has been heard on the island, the brunette says, "Do you think our friend has forgotten us? I am a very good swimmer and I am sure I can make it to the mainland. As soon I get ashore I promise I will get help for you." Off goes the brunette. She is a stronger swimmer, but she is also unlucky, because the wind is the in the wrong direction. She gets three-quarters of the way across before exhaustion gets the better of her and she too drowns. The blonde waits a couple of days for help to arrive, but of course, no one appears. Faced with the prospect of dying of starvation, alone on the island, or trying to swim for it, she decides to try to swim. Her luck is in because the wind has turned around and she quickly gets to within a half-kilometre of the shore. At this point she remembers that she left the fire burning on the island, so she turns back to put it out.

****

Animal
Crackers

Beastly
jokes

A tiny zoo in Suffolk is given a very rare species of gorilla by an eccentric explorer. After a couple of weeks, the gorilla starts to go wild: it won't eat, can't sleep, becomes violent and causes all sorts of problems. The zoo owner calls the vet, determines that the gorilla is a female and, what's more, she's on heat. The only way to calm her down is to have someone mate with her. Sadly, there are no other gorillas of her species in captivity, so another solution will have to be found. It is then that the owner remembers Richard, the cage cleaner. Richard is a bit dumb, but he has a reputation for having sex with anything, so the owner decides to offer him a proposition: would he like to have sex with the gorilla for £500? Richard says he's interested, but that he'll need the night to think it over. The next day he says he'd be willing and that he'd accept the offer, but only if the owner meets three conditions. "First," he says, "I don't want to kiss her on the lips." The owner says that's fine. "Second," Richard says, "you must never, ever tell anyone about this." That's fine, the owner says again. "And third," says Richard, "I'm going to need another week to come up with the money."

****

A pig farmer is worried because none of his pigs are getting pregnant. His pigs are his livelihood, so he calls the vet and asks him what on earth he can do to make them procreate. The vet says that if the pigs really won't do the business he should try artificial insemination. The farmer doesn't have a clue what artificial insemination is, but he reckons it must mean he has to get the pigs pregnant by himself. So he loads them all into his truck, drives them to the woods and shags them all. The next day he calls the vet again and asks him how he will be able to tell if his pigs are pregnant. The vet tells him that the pigs will be lying down rolling in mud. The farmer looks out of the window and sees that all his pigs are really clean and all standing up in their field. So he herds them into his truck, drives them to the woods and shags them all again. The next morning the farmer gets up and looks at the pig field. All the pigs are still clean and all standing. So the farmer herds them yet again into his truck, drives them to the woods and shags them all. Early the next morning the farmer is exhausted so he asks his wife to have a look at the pigs to see if they are rolling in mud. His wife gets up, looks out at the pig field and says, "That's very odd: the pigs are all in your truck. Two of them are waving over here and one's tooting the horn!"

****

Four dog owners were having a post-walk drink together on a Friday, and were all boasting about the merits of their dogs. The first man was an engineer. "Set-square! Set-square – do your thing!" he said to his dog. Set-square leapt up and ran over to the desk, opened a drawer, took out some paper, a pen and a set square. He took it all over to the table and proceeded to draw a careful circle, triangle and some perfect parallel lines on the paper. There was a round of applause, but the second man – an accountant – insisted his dog could do better. "Slide-rule! Slide-rule – do your thing!" he said to his dog. Slide-rule trotted off to the kitchen and came back with a tin of biscuits. He opened them on the table, counted out 12 and then divided those into four piles of three. He pushed one pile towards each man and took the tin back to the kitchen. There was a round of applause, but the third man – a chemist – insisted his dog could do better. "Measuring-cup! Measuring-cup – do your thing!" he said to his dog. Measuring-cup ran into the kitchen and came back with three cans of beer and four glasses. He opened all the beers and poured them evenly into the glasses without spilling a drop. There was a round of applause and the fourth man – a civil servant – said his dog could do better. "Tea-break! Tea-break! Do your thing!" the man shouted loudly. After a lengthy pause, Tea-break leapt up, ate the biscuits, drank the beer, had a crap on the paper, groped up the other dogs, claimed he hurt himself while doing so, filed a complaint to the union for unsafe working conditions and went home sick!

****

A fly was hovering over a lake. A fish, swimming below the water, saw the fly and said to itself, "If that fly would just drop six more inches, I could get it." In the woods beside the lake, a bear was watching the fish and said to itself, "If that fly would just drop six more inches, the fish could get that fly and I could get that fish." Deeper in the woods, a hunter, sitting eating a sandwich, saw the bear and said to himself, "If that fly would just drop six more inches, that fish could get that fly, that bear could get that fish and I could get that bear." Just behind him a mouse was watching. The mouse said to itself, "If that fly would just drop six more inches, that fish could get that fly, that bear could get that fish, that hunter could get that bear and I could get that sandwich." Behind the mouse was a cat, watching intently. It said to itself, "If that fly would just drop six more inches, that fish could get that fly, that bear could get that fish, that hunter could get that bear, that mouse could get that sandwich and I could get that mouse!" Suddenly, the fly dropped six inches. The fish leaped up and snapped it up. The bear grabbed the fish, and the hunter jumped up and shot the bear. The mouse leaped for the sandwich and the cat jumped for the mouse, but was too excited, so shot past it and landed in the lake. The moral of the story? Every time a fly drops six inches, a pussy gets wet!

****

A man decided he wanted to become a hunter, so he set about getting himself all the equipment. Last on his list was a dog, so he went off to see the local dog breeder. The dog breeder took him out to the woods with hos best dog so the man could see what a top hunting dog it was. The dog breeder snapped his fingers at the dog and shouted, "Go!" The dog ran off at top speed and they could hear much crashing in the undergrowth. The dog came running back, out of breath, and barked once. "What does that mean?" said the man. "One bark means that the dog saw one rabbit in the woods," said the dog breeder. The man thought this was cool, but that he'd better see it again in case it was a scam. Again, the dog merchant snapped his fingers and shouted, "Go!" The dog ran off at top speed and they could hear more crashing of undergrowth. The dog came running back, out of breath, and barked twice. "What does that mean?" said the man. "Two barks mean that the dog saw two rabbits in the woods," said the dog breeder. The man asked to see it one more time, and the dog breeder snapped his fingers at the dog and shouted, "Go!" The dog disappeared again, but this time he came back carrying a stick and began to hump the dog breeder's leg. "What the hell does that mean?" asked the man, astonished. "Well, that means he just saw more effing rabbits than you can shake a stick at!"

****

A jaguar was walking pugnaciously through the jungle, intimidating the other animals. He spotted a monkey and ran up to it, pinning it against the trunk of a tree. "Who is the fiercest animal in the jungle?" he roared. "You: you are," the monkey squeaked. Satisfied, the jaguar let him go and carried on, noticing with satisfaction that all the other animals were running away from him. He nonetheless managed to immobilize a bird and growled in a terrifying manner: "Who is the fiercest animal in the jungle?" 'You: you are," the bird stammered, and the jaguar magnanimously let him go. The jaguar then spotted a lion having a siesta and, giddy with self-importance, made the mistake of running up to him. "Who is the fiercest animal in the jungle?" he roared, eyes bulging. Hearing this, the lion stood up, picked up the jaguar by the tail, swung him around faster and faster and finally released him and sent him crashing heavily into a banana tree. "All right, all right," the jaguar said, standing up groggily and shaking his head to clear it. "Even if you don't know the answer, it's no reason to get pissed off."

****

A horse and a chicken are friends. They are playing around together one day when the horse tumbles into a pit and begins to sink. He begs the chicken to fetch the farmer to get him to pull him to safety. The chicken runs off but he cannot find the farmer. Ever resourceful, the chicken jumps into the farmer's Porsche (obviously a French farmer, full of EU subsidies) and roars off to the hole where the horse is rapidly sinking. He takes a tow-rope from the boot, ties it around the bumper and throws the other end to the horse. The horse manages to grip the rope in his teeth and the chicken pulls forward in the Porsche, thus pulling the horse from danger and saving his life. A couple of days later the horse and the chicken are playing the same game in the same place. This time, the chicken falls into the same hole and begins to sink. The chicken screams for help and the horse, even more resourceful than the chicken, straddles himself over the hole, positioning his penis over where the chicken is sinking. "Quick, chicken," he says. "Grab hold of this and pull yourself out!" The chicken follows his instructions and only a few seconds later, both animals are safely on solid ground. The moral of the story? If you're hung like a horse, you don't need a Porsche to pull the birds!

****

Hillary Clinton goes into a pet shop and sees the most beautiful parrot she has ever seen. "Does it talk?" she enquires of the shopkeeper. "He sure does, ma'am," the man replies. "Well, how come he only costs fifty bucks when all the other parrots are at least five hundred?" "Well, ma'am, that's a good question, and the answer is that he's got a bit of a fruity vocabulary on him. He used to live in a brothel and some of the things he says would even make a tart blush!" Hillary, used to foul language and deeds, says, "Not a problem for me. I'll take him right now." She gets home and places the parrot in its new cage in the front room. The parrot turns to her as soon as the cover goes off the cage, looks her square in the eye and says, "New house, new madam!" Hillary laughs and carries on with her day. Later on, Chelsea arrives with a friend and they go over to pet the new bird. The parrot turns to them, looks them square in the eye, and squawks, "New house, new whores." They run off, giggling. Later that night, Bill comes home after a hard day's work. He walks up to have a look at the new bird. The parrot turns to him, and with the briefest glance says, "Hey, Bill!"

****

A plane crashes and five men are stranded on a desert island. They are all in their early 20s and very horny. After a month of survival John gets up and says, "I can't take it any more: I'm so horny I'm going to shag that female gorilla at the other end of the island." He grabs himself a bag and runs off. The other four guys follow him and they quickly catch the gorilla. Each of the guys grabs a limb and John pops the bag over its head, jumps on top of the animal and starts to screw it. The gorilla is pretty strong and doesn't put up with any nonsense, so pretty soon it gets an arm clear, and then another. It puts both of them around John's waist and holds on tight. Then it gets first one, then the other leg free as well. and it wraps both of them around John, too. The gorilla seems to be enjoying itself and John starts to shout, "Get it off! Get it off!" One of his mates says, "You must be joking: you're on top and she's wrapped around you tightly." John says, "Not the gorilla – I mean the bag: I want to kiss her!"

****

A farmer has a prize cock which has sired hundreds of young. It used to take care of every single one of the farmer's 200 chickens. But one day the old cock dies and the farmer is forced to get himself a replacement. The farmer looks at all the ads in *Farmers' Weekly* and orders a mail-order rooster named Randy. A couple of days later the new cock arrives. It is a very impressive and fit-looking bird. Before the farmer lets the rooster loose to work on his chickens, he gives it a bit of a pep talk. "Now, look here, Randy," the farmer says, "I need you as a long-term investment. I don't need a new rooster for just the next couple of days: I need one for a very long time. So take it easy and pace yourself when you get in there, OK?" Randy nods and the farmer puts him into the coop. But no sooner have Randy's claws hit the ground than he is off at the first brace of hens. The farmer looks on amazed as he sees the rooster making his way through the entire flock, doing all of the hens first once and then twice! The rooster doesn't even pause for breath. When he's done, he looks around and sees a load of ducks out by the pond. He sprints over and does them too – twice each. The farmer, while obviously impressed, is worried that his superb new rooster won't even make it through the night if he's that horny already. The farmer's worst fears are confirmed the next morning when he leaves the house after breakfast: Randy is lying a hundred yards from the hencoop with buzzards circling around him. The farmer, shaking his head, walks slowly up to the chicken and looks down at him. "What the hell did I tell you, Randy?" he begins, "I knew you wouldn't make it if you didn't pace yourself!" Randy opens one eye and looks up at the farmer, then up at the buzzards. "Sshhhh," he says. "They're getting closer!"

****

A koala bear escapes from the zoo, decides to get himself a night out on the town and chances upon a prostitute. He spends the entire night with her, but every time they have sex he stops to eat a sandwich. The prostitute is a little surprised but figures, "Hey, I'm having sex with a koala bear, so what the heck?" In the morning the bear gets up, has a shower and is starting to walk out of the door when the prostitute calls him back. "Aren't you forgetting something, honey?" she asks. The bear turns around, looks at her and shrugs his shoulders. She realizes he doesn't understand so she beckons him back and gets a dictionary. In it, she looks up the word "prostitute" and the definition is, "Someone who has sex and gets paid for it." The koala understands, but picks up the dictionary and flicks to the "koala" definition. It says simply, "Eats shoots and leaves."

****

Once upon a time, there was a beautiful, independent princess who was very self-assured. One day she was walking in the forest when she chanced upon a frog sitting on a rock in a stream. To her amazement, the frog begins to talk to her: "Fair princess, I am a handsome prince, trapped by a witch in the foul, slimy body of this poor frog. Won't you kiss me once to break the spell and we can live happily ever after in my castle with my mother and my father and my knights and you can bear my children and look after them and prepare my meals and clean my sheets and all will be well?" That night, as the beautiful, independent princess ate her frog's legs, she thought to herself and laughed out loud: "Not this time!"

****

At primary school one day, the teacher was reading the *Three Little Pigs* to her youngest class. When she got to the part about the pig building his house from straw she read, "And the little pig went to the farmer and said, 'Please mister farmer can I have some straw to build my house with?'" And then the teacher asked the whole class, "And what do you think the farmer said?" Little Johnny in the corner put up his hand and said, "I know, miss. He said, 'Blow me – a talking pig!'"

****

A Welshman is shipwrecked after a big storm and ends up on a desert island with only an Alsatian and a sheep for company. There is enough food for them all and there is plentiful fresh water, too. The weather is great and they all have a pretty good time. After a few months, the three of them get into the habit of walking up into the hills to watch the sun go down every night. One particularly balmy night, everything is just beautiful: the sea can be heard gently lapping in the distance, the cool breeze carries the sound of the crickets chirping and everyone is happy. The Welshman looks over at the sheep and the sheep looks back. They glance into each other's eyes and the Welshman starts to feel warm inside. The sheep continues to look at him, so he reaches out and puts his arm around the animal. As soon as he does this, the Alsatian begins to growl, and doesn't stop until the arm is removed. The three of them continue to watch the sunset, but there is no more funny business. After a few more weeks there is a huge storm and a beautiful woman is washed up on the beach. She is pretty ill and has to be tended night and day for weeks before she even has enough strength to talk. After a few months of tender, loving care the woman is perfectly well again and the four of them all get along fine. The Welshman, the sheep and the Alsatian introduce the woman to their nightly ritual of watching the sun go down, and one night they are all there and it is just magical. As before, they can hear the sea, smell the scented air and see the most beautiful sunset of their lives and as before, romance is most certainly in the air. The Welshman is getting his warm feeling inside so he turns to the beautiful, scantily-clad maiden at his side and just nuzzles his mouth up next to her ear. She tips her head to one side to hear what he has to say, as he whispers, "You wouldn't take the dog off for a walk, would you?"

****

An old man walks into a bar using a cane and carrying a crocodile. The barman says, "Sorry, mate, no animals allowed in here – especially dangerous ones like that." The man says, "Oh, go on: my croc can do a fantastic trick and it'll have people coming from miles around to see it. Let me show you." "Well, OK then," says the barman, "but if I think it's crap I'm going to chuck the pair of you out." So the old man says something to the croc, who gets up on his hind legs and opens his mouth. The man then drops his trousers and puts his pecker into the croc's mouth. The croc shuts its mouth tight around his pecker. The crowd in the bar all gasp out loud, but then the man picks up his cane and raps the croc's head with it three times – tap, tap, tap! The croc opens its mouth and the man's pecker is there – still attached – without even a scratch on it. Everyone in the bar starts clapping and cheering the old man. "Now," says the man looking around the bar, "Does anybody else think they're up to this fantastic trick? Would anyone else like a go?" There is silence and all the men look to the floor. Suddenly an old lady pipes up, "I'll have a try, but you only need to hit me on the head once!"

****

A guy walks into his local with a giraffe and a monkey. All three of them get utterly blotto. The man and and the monkey manage to prop each other up and make it to the door, but the giraffe is too big for them to help and he collapses on the floor. As the man opens the door the barman shouts across the bar, "Oi, mate, you can't leave that lyin' there!" and the man shouts back, "That's no lion – it's a giraffe and I can't move him!"

****

A local business was looking to employ someone to help in the office. The manager put a sign in the window saying: "Help wanted. Must be able to type, good with a computer and bilingual. We are an Equal Opportunities Employer." Soon afterwards a dog trotted up to the window, saw the sign and went inside. He looked at the receptionist and wagged his tail, then walked over to the sign, looked at it and barked sharply. Getting the idea, the receptionist fetched the office manager, who looked at the dog with surprise. However, the dog looked determined, so he led him into his office. Inside, the dog jumped up on a chair and stared at the manager. The manager said, in as friendly a tone as possible, "I can't hire you. The sign says you have to be able to type." The dog jumped down, went to the typewriter and proceeded to type out a perfect letter. He took out the page in his mouth and gave it to the manager, then jumped back onto the chair. The manager was stunned, but then told the dog, "The sign says you have to be good with a computer." The dog jumped down again and went to the computer. The dog proceeded to demonstrate his expertise with various programs. After a few minutes he produced a sample spreadsheet and database and presented them to the manager. By this time the manager was totally dumbfounded. He looked at the dog and said, "I realize that you are a very intelligent dog and have some interesting abilities. However, I still can't give you the job." The dog jumped down and went to a copy of the sign and put his paw on the part about being an Equal Opportunities Employer. The manager said, "Yes, I know, but the sign also says that you have to be bilingual." The dog looked at him straight in the face, and said: "Miaow."

****

A little old lady had two monkeys as pets for years. One day, one of them died of natural causes. Overcome with grief, the second monkey passed away two days later. Not knowing what to do with the remains, she finally decided to take them to the taxidermist and have them stuffed. After telling the owner of her wishes, he asked her, "Do you want them mounted?" "No. Holding hands will be fine," she said, blushing.

****

Two tall trees, a birch and a beech, are growing in the woods. A small tree begins to grow between them. One tree says to the other: "Is that a son of a beech or a son of a birch?" The other says he cannot tell. Just then a woodpecker lands in the sapling. The tall tree asks: "Woodpecker, you're a tree expert. Can you tell if that's a son of a beech or a son of a birch?" The woodpecker takes a taste of the small tree. He replies: "It is neither a son of a beech nor a son of a birch. That, my friends, is the best piece of ash I have ever put my pecker in."

****

Deep in the forest, a tortoise was slowly padding towards a tall tree. Ever so slowly she started climbing the tree. After a few days of this, she managed to climb high enough to reach the lowest branch, but it was apparently not high enough, as she carried on upwards. It took her a week to reach a suitable branch and then another three days to arrive at the end of the branch. Once there, she took a deep breath and hurled herself forward, instantly falling like a brick all the way down, finishing her trip with a thud in the dirt below. A couple of birds had been watching the whole process for a week and the male bird turned to his mate and chirped: "Dear, I know how much this will upset you, but we'll have to tell her she's adopted."

****

This guy had been dating this girl for some time when she invited him over to her parents' house for dinner to meet them. When they got there, the guy realized he was so tense that he was starting to get really bad gas. They sat down for dinner but he just couldn't hold it in any longer. A fart slipped out. The mother yelled "Spot!" The guy realized the family dog was under his chair, and was relieved that the dog had got the blame. A few minutes later he let another one go and the mother again yelled "Spot!" Again, the boyfriend was relieved that the dog had been told off, so he decided he might as well get it all out, and let this huge fart go. "Spot!" the mother yelled. "Get out from under there before he shits on you!"

****

A team of elephants had agreed to play a game of football against a team of ants. Things were going well for the ants – more agile and more nimble than the elephants – when the referee whistled loudly. Everybody from both teams gathered around the remains of an unfortunate ant, now completely squashed to bits on the pitch. "There you are," an ant complained bitterly. "You just can't trust the big people to play fair!" "I didn't want this to happen," the elephant said guiltily. "I just wanted to trip him over."

****

A frog goes into a London bank and approaches the teller. He can see from her nameplate that the teller's name is Patricia Whack. He says, "Ms Whack, I'd like to get a loan to buy a boat and go on a long vacation." Patti looks at the frog in disbelief and asks how much he wants to borrow. The frog says £30,000. The teller asks his name and the frog says that his name is Kermit Jagger and that it's OK, he knows the bank manager. Patti explains that £30,000 is a substantial amount of money and that he will need to secure the loan. She asks if he has anything he can use as collateral. The frog says, "Sure. I have this," and he produces a tiny pink porcelain elephant, about half an inch tall. It's bright pink and perfectly formed, but of no obvious visible value. Very confused, Patti explains that she'll have to consult with the manager and disappears into a back office. She finds the manager and reports: "There's a frog called Kermit Jagger out there who claims to know you, and he wants to borrow £30,000. He wants to use this as collateral," she says, holding up the tiny pink elephant. "I mean, what the heck is this?" The bank manager looks back at her and says: "It's a knick-knack, Patti Whack. Give the frog a loan. His old man's a Rolling Stone!"

****

An old man had a dog he just loved but this dog had the nasty habit of attacking anything that moved, including people. His friends told him if he had the dog "fixed", he would lose his aggression and quit this behaviour. Thinking it might be a good idea, the old man had his dog fixed. A few days later he was in his front room when the postman came up the steps. The dog jumped up, went right through the door and attacked the postman. The old man ran out, pulled his dog away and began apologizing. "I am so sorry," he said. "I don't know what to do or say. My friends told me he would quit attacking people if I had him fixed, but it didn't work. I just don't know what to do." The postman picked himself up and said, "You should have had his teeth pulled: I knew when he came through the door he wasn't going to screw me."

****

It was Frank's first time at bear hunting. After some time in the mountains, he spotted a small brown bear and shot it. Just then there was a tap on his shoulder. He turned around to see a big black bear. The bear said: "You've got two choices. I either maul you to death or we have sex." Frank decided to bend over. Even though he felt sore for two weeks, Frank soon recovered and vowed revenge. He headed out on another trip where he found the black bear and shot it. There was another tap on his shoulder. This time a huge grizzly bear stood right next to him. The grizzly said: "What a huge mistake, Frank. You've got two choices. Either I maul you to death or we have rough sex." Again, Frank thought it was better to comply. Although he survived, it took several months before Frank finally recovered. Outraged, he headed back to the mountains, managed to track down the grizzly and shot it. He felt sweet revenge, but then there was a tap on his shoulder. He turned round to find a giant polar bear standing there. The polar bear said: "Admit it, Frank. You don't come here for the hunting, do you?"

****

Two young nuns, freshly inducted into their order, were visiting the zoo when they stopped in front of the gorilla cage. Something about them made the gorilla mad with desire and, after beating his chest for a while, he ran to the bars of the cage, pulled them open, jumped on one of the nuns and ravished her before going back into his cage, contented. The nun picked herself up, brushed down her clothes and said to her friend: "Promise me never to talk about this – ever." To which the other sister agreed. Twenty-five years later, the two sisters found themselves together again and went to sit on a bench in a nearby park. "I know I promised never to talk about this incident," the nun said, "but there's a question I've always wanted to ask you…" "All right: ask your question, sister." "Did it hurt?" "Did it hurt?" the nun replied in a sad voice. "Oh, yes, it hurt. He never called… he never wrote… he never sent flowers…"

****

A ventriloquist is on a walking holiday in Wales and getting pretty bored. During one of his walks he stumbles across a farm and there, leaning on a gate, is a farmer, so the ventriloquist decides to have a bit of fun. "Hey, cool dog you have here, sir. Mind if I speak to him?" "My dog doesn't talk," the farmer says, surprised. "Hey, dog, how's it going?" the ventriloquist asks the dog. "Doin' alright." the dog says. The farmer stares at his dog in total disbelief, as he can't believe man's best friend can talk. "This is your owner, right?" the prankster asks the dog, pointing at the farmer. "Yep," says the dog. "How is he treating you?" "Real good. He walks me twice a day, feeds me great food and takes me to the lake once a week to play." The farmer is still shocked, starting to feel bad over rubbing his dog's nose into his own poop after last week's potty incident. "Mind if I talk to your horse?" the ventriloquist then asks. "Hey?" blurts the farmer. "My horse doesn't talk." The ventriloquist approaches the horse: "Hey, horse, how's it going?" "Cool," says the horse. "Is this your owner?" "Yep," says the horse. "How's he treating you?" "Pretty good, thanks for asking. He rides me regularly, brushes me down often and keeps me in the barn to protect me from the elements." By this time, the farmer is completely amazed and his eyes are bulging out of their sockets. The ventriloquist approaches the gate and says: "Mind if I talk to your sheep?" The farmer coughs loudly and says quickly: "Sheep lie!"

****

Two whales, a male and a female, are swimming happily through the ocean. On seeing a boat, the male says to his friend: "Hey, I've got a great idea! Let's swim up under that boat and blow out really hard through our blowholes!" The female says, "Uh… I don't know…" "Come on, it'll be fun: just this once!" The female agrees and they swim up under the boat and blow out, capsizing the boat and sending the hapless sailors into the water. As they are swimming away, the male says, "Wow! That was fun, wasn't it? Hey! I've got another idea! Let's swim back there and eat all the sailors!" The female, exasperated, replies, "Look, I agreed to the blow job, but I'm not swallowing any seamen."

****

An ant and an elephant share a night of romance. Next morning the ant wakes up and the elephant is dead. "Damn," says the ant. "One night of passion and I spend the rest of my life digging a grave!"

****

A city man, completely ignorant of country life, was visiting Wales. He stopped at an educational farm, had a look around and went to chat with the farmer. "Nice pigs you've got there," he said. "How big are they?" The pig farmer puts one of the pig's tails in his mouth and bobbed his head up and down. "30 pounds," he said to the city guy. "What? I can't believe that's the way you weigh pigs! You're having me on!" "No, I'm not," the farmer said. He then called his son over and asked him to weigh the pig. The son put the pig's tail in his mouth, bobbed his head a couple of times and said the pig weighed 30 pounds. As the city guy still couldn't believe this was the way to weigh a pig, the farmer asked his son to go and get his mum so that she could weigh the pig, too. The boy left and came back alone a few minutes later, saying: "Mum can't come: she's busy weighing the postman."

****

Mama Weevil gave birth to two identical twin weevils. They grew up together, but there came a time when they had to discover the world on their own, and tearfully they separated, each to go its own weevil way. One was very successful in Hollywood, got tons of girlfriends and money, while the other didn't have much luck in its life and ended up broke, alone and miserable. He was, therefore, known as the lesser of two weevils.

****

A fisherman accidentally left his day's catch under the seat of a bus. The next evening's newspaper carried an ad: "If the person who left a bucket of fish on the number 47 bus would care to come to the garage, he can have the bus."

****

A mother and baby camel were talking one day when the baby camel asked, "Mum, why have I got these huge three-toed feet?" "Well, son, when we trek across the desert your toes will help you to stay on top of the soft sand," the mother replied, "OK," said the son. A few minutes later, the son asked, "Mum, why have I got these great long eyelashes?" "They are there to keep the sand out of your eyes on the trips through the desert." "Thanks, Mum," replied the son, and went off to think on his own. After a short while, the son returned and asked, "Mum, why have I got these great big humps on my back?" The mother, now a little impatient with the boy, replied, "They're to help us store water for our long treks across the desert, so we can go without drinking for long periods." "That's great, Mum: so we have huge feet to stop us sinking, and long eyelashes to keep the sand from our eyes and these humps to store water. But Mum…" "Yes, son?" "Why the heck are we in London Zoo?"

✱✱✱✱

Two vultures board an aeroplane, each carrying two dead raccoons. The stewardess looks at them and says, "I'm sorry, gentlemen, only one carrion per passenger."

✱✱✱✱

A three-legged dog walks into a saloon in the Old West. He slides up to the bar and announces: "I'm looking for the man who shot my paw."

✱✱✱✱

A wolf had been chasing a rabbit in the forest for an hour when they arrived near the Enchanted Oak, where the genie lived… They were making such a racket that they woke up the genie, who said (he was a bit of a hippy): "OK, OK: I see that there is no sleeping in peace in here until you two have resolved your differences. Therefore, I am going to grant you three wishes and you'll go on your way much happier." The wolf had the first go and he said: "I want all the wolves in this forest to be female." The genie sighed and said that it now was so. He turned to the rabbit and said: "What is your first wish, rabbit?" "I'd like a helmet," the rabbit says, a faint smile on his face. The genie finds it a bit odd, but a wish is a wish and the rabbit is fitted with a nice crash-helmet. "I want all the wolves in this country to be female," says the wolf for his second wish. The genie sighs again but complies and all the wolves in the country become female. "For my second wish, I want a motorcycle," the rabbit says. The genie says "OK" and grants the rabbit a nice, powerful motorbike which goes very well with the helmet. The rabbit's smile is getting bigger now. True to his character and showing remarkable consistency, the wolf says: "For my third wish, I want all the wolves in the whole *world* to be female!" Marvelling at the single-mindedness of the wolf's wishes, the genie complies and turns all the wolves in the world female. He then turns to the rabbit, who is grinning from ear to ear. "So what is your last wish, rabbit?" The rabbit straps the helmet on his head securely, climbs on the motorbike, revs up the engine and says: "I wish the wolf was gay!"

****

Why do cows have bells?
Because their horns don't work.

****

A labrador, a rottweiler and a chihuahua spot a nice-looking female poodle. They rush to meet her and the poodle, aware of her charms, pouts coquettishly and tells them: "I will go out with the one of you who can use the words 'liver' and 'cheese' in a proper sentence." The labrador goes first, racks his brains and blurts out: "I like liver and cheese." "What imagination!" giggles the poodles. The rottweiler growls and prances, then says lamely: "I hate liver and I hate cheese." "That's even worse than the labrador!" howls the poodle in glee. Then the chihuahua winks at her and says: "Liver alone. Cheese mine."

****

A duck enters a grocery store and says to the man behind the counter: "Do you have any beer?" "I'm sorry, but this is a grocery store. We're not licensed to sell beer here." The duck leaves, but comes back the next day. "Do you have any beer?" he asks. "I told you yesterday! We don't sell beer here! This is a grocery store! If you come here again asking for beer, I'll nail your feet to the floor!" The duck leaves, but comes back the next day. "Do you have any nails?" The shop owner says: "No." The duck continues, "Do you have any any beer?"

****

A burglar breaks into a house really late one night. He spies a nice new DVD player in the front room and starts to walk over to it when he hears the words, "Jesus is watching you." He jumps but stays in place and holds his breath. There is no more sound so the burglar takes another step forward. As he does so, he hears again, "Jesus is watching you!" He jumps again and looks around the room again. In one of the corners he sees what looks like a cage. He goes over to it and sees a parrot inside, looking at him. "Was that you talking about Jesus?" the man asks the parrot. "It sure was," says the parrot. The burglar relaxes and feels a whole lot better. "So, what's your name then parrot?" he asks the parrot. "Arbuthenot" says the parrot. The burglar laughs and says, "What a dumb name, who on earth named you that?" The parrot replies, "the same person who named the doberman Jesus!"

****

Two cows were standing in a field. One cow says to the other, "Moooooo." The other says, "I was just going to say that."

****

Why do gorillas have big nostrils?
Because they have big fingers.

****

What's yellow and smells like bananas?
Monkey vomit.

****

A man was walking on the sidewalk and noticed up ahead that little Johnny was wearing a red fireman's hat and sitting in a red wagon. It appeared that the wagon was being pulled slowly by a large labrador retriever. When he got closer to the lad, he noticed that Johnny had a rope tied around the dog's testicles, which probably accounted for why the dog was walking so gingerly. Smiling, he spoke to the little boy, "That's really a nice fire engine you have there, son, but I'll bet the dog would pull you faster if you tied that rope around his neck." "Yeah," little Johnny replied, "but then I wouldn't have a siren."

****

A bloke was about to bring his new girlfriend home, so he warned his parrot not to make any offensive remarks; the parrot had a tendency to verbally abuse anyone who came into the house. The next night the guy walked in with his new girlfriend, and the parrot instantly began to insult her: "Who's a fat cow, then? Who's been hit by a truck, then?" The next day, the infuriated man decided to shove the parrot in the freezer to teach it a lesson. About two minutes later the parrot called out, "I'm sorry. I'm really sorry. I'm really, really sorry. I won't do it again!" The man let the parrot back out and said: "I hope you behave, otherwise it's back in the cooler!" For the next couple of months he didn't hear so much as a squeak out of the parrot. He couldn't believe how successful his freezer trick turned out to be. But finally one night the parrot got up enough courage to talk again. "Excuse me, please," the parrot said, very cautiously, "but what exactly did the chicken do?"

****

Two mice walk into a bar for a few ales when a giraffe walks in. "Look at that. She's a beauty," says one mouse. "Well, why not try your luck?" his friend suggests. So the mouse goes over to the giraffe and starts talking to her, and within five minutes they're out the door and gone into the night. Next day, the second mouse is in the bar drinking away, when his friend staggers in. The mouse is absolutely stuffed, worn out, ruined – an ex-mouse. The mouse helps his pal up on to a stool, pours a drink down his throat and asks: "What the hell happened to you? I saw you leave with the giraffe: what happened after that? Was she all right?" The first mouse says: "Yeah, she was really something else. We went out to dinner, had a couple of glasses of wine and she invited me back to her place to spend the night. And oh, man! I've never had a night like it!" "But how come you look like you're so exhausted?" "Well," says the mouse, "between the kissing and the screwing, I must have run a thousand miles!"

****

A farmer decides it's time to get a new cock to look after his hens. The old one is a bit of a ragbag and, despite doing a reasonable job, the farmer figures he hasn't got all that long to go, so he may as well replace him sooner rather than later. He buys a new cock and lets him out in the barnyard to mix it up with the hens and sort it out with the old rooster. Now, the old rooster is pretty wise, and not the sort to take anything lying down, so he thinks to himself, "I'll have the last laugh here: I'm not ready to become lunch and dinner quite yet." So he walks up to the new cock and says, "So you think you're good enough to take over, then, do you? Well, I'll tell you what: instead of fighting and all that stuff, if you can beat me in a simple running race – just ten times around that old hen-house – I'll just leave quietly and not cause any fuss at all. I'll leave all the hens to you." "Old man, you've got yourself a deal," says the young rooster, puffing himself up and checking himself out in a mirror. "I'll even tell you what," continues the youngster with growing confidence, "you can have a half-lap head start – I know I'm going to win, after all!" So the race starts with the old rooster a good half lap in front of the younger one. The old one has still got some strength left so he keeps a good pace for the first lap – he's not lost any distance. By the end of the second lap he is flagging just a little and by the end of the third the young rooster is noticeably gaining on him. By the time the fourth lap is over the old cock's lead has slipped seriously and at the end of the fifth the younger rooster can reach out and touch the older one. Still they run. At this point the farmer hears some noise from the chicken run. He walks out of the house, does a double-take, runs back in again and comes out with his shotgun. He stands and looks at the two roosters running for all they are worth around the hen-house, takes aim and BANG! blows the young rooster away. As he turns and walks away he mutters to himself, "Unbelievable: that's the third gay rooster I've bought in as many weeks!"

****

One day a lion was walking around the jungle, sad, lonely and bored stiff, when he spotted a monkey high up in a tree. He yelled up to the monkey to come down and play, but the monkey was too scared. So the lion asked the monkey what he could do to make him feel comfortable enough to come down. The monkey said, "If you tie yourself up, I'll come down." The lion tied himself up, but as the monkey came down he started shaking. The lion said: "Hey, monkey, you don't have to be scared! I'm not going to eat you; I'm tied up real tight." "I know," said the monkey. "That's not why I'm shaking." "Why are you shaking, then?" "It's the excitement," explains the monkey. "I've never fucked a lion before."

****

Did you know sharks will only attack you if you're wet?

****

A man was out walking his pit bull and decided to stop in the local tavern for a quick beer. Some time later, a second man entered the establishment and asked: "Who owns the pit bull outside?" The first man answers: "I do. Why?" The second man says: "Well, my pet chihuahua's out there killing it." "What rubbish! I don't believe it!" the first man says. "Suit yourself, but he's choking to death on it."

****

A penguin is on holiday in Arizona. He's driving around the desert when he sees the oil light on his car light up. He quickly stops at the next garage, just up the road. He asks the mechanic if he can take a look at the car and the mechanic says he can but he'll have to do a couple of other things first, so could the penguin leave the car and come back soon? "Sure," says the penguin and he goes off to find an ice cream parlour thinking that, as a penguin in Arizona, a bowl of ice cream will cool him down nicely. Having no hands, it's not easy to eat ice cream if you're a penguin, so he ends up covered in ice cream and has to hurry back to the garage to see what's up with his car. He asks the mechanic what's up with it and the mechanic replies, "It looks like you've blown a seal." The penguin, shocked, says, "No, no: it's just ice cream, I promise!"

****

Why did the turkey cross the road twice?
To prove he wasn't chicken.

****

A non-too-bright zebra escaped from a zoo and ended up in a field full of cows. He walked up to one and said: "Hi there! What do you do around here then?" "I eat grass all day and get milked morning and night," replied the cow. "Oh," the zebra said. He walked idly about and met another cow. "Hi there! Say, what do you do around here then?" he asked again. "I eat grass all day and get milked morning and night," replied the cow. The zebra nodded, pleased by the quietness and the sense of purpose of the cows' lives, then walked over to a bull. "Hello," he said. "What do you do around here?" The bull looked him up and down and said: "Get those pyjamas off and I'll show you."

****

Forgive Me Father

9

Jokes for the
faithful

A man is rushed to his nearest hospital in New York, Our Holy Mother of BeJesus, after a heart attack. The surgeon performs heart surgery and the man survives no problem. Afterwards, the man is lying in his bed and one of the nuns is comforting him. "Don't worry sir, you'll be just fine, it's all over now," says the nun. "But we would like to know, sir, if you don't mind the asking, as to how you intend to pay your bill for the operation and the care. Would you be covered by an insurance policy?" "Well, actually sister, I don't think I am," the man replies. "Oh dear," continues the nun, "maybe you've got a load of money lying around and you'd like to pay by cash?" "Er, no I don't think so sister," the man replies. "I'm not really a man of much material wealth." "Well," says the nun, "perhaps you've some close family who could help out?" "Well not really sister," the man replies, "I've just the one sister in County Kerry in the old country, but she's a spinster nun." The nun replies, "Nuns are not spinsters, sir, nuns are married to God." "In that case," says the man, "perhaps you could get my brother-in-law to foot the bill!"

****

Two nuns walk into an off-license and pick up the biggest bottle of whisky that they can find. When they get to the cashdesk the salesman says, "I'm not sure that I can sell booze to you ladies now can I? I didn't think you were supposed to drink that stuff." "Don't be worrying yourself about that now will you," replies one of the sisters, "it's not for lowly nuns like us, 'tis for the Holy Mother Superior –

she has constipation!" "Oh well sister," says the salesman, "I'm so sorry, in that case, have the bottle on the house and wish her my best." The nuns thank him and leave quietly. A couple of hours later the salesman shuts up the shop and leaves. As he is walking to the bus stop he hears laughing and sees the two nuns sitting on a park bench laughing their heads off, rolling around and drinking all the whisky he gave them. He is disgusted and runs over to them. "You lied to me sisters!" he begins, "you told me that whisky was for the Holy Mother Superior's constipation." "And so it is," replies one of the nuns, "and so it is – when the Holy Mother Superior sees us in this state she's sure to shit herself!"

****

Brother William is on his way back from teaching children at a local school. It is late at night and the Abbey's car that he is travelling in breaks down. He knows that he hasn't run out of petrol because he's just filled up, so he opens up the bonnet and starts to have a look at the engine. A few minutes later a car pulls up next to him and the window is wound down. A red-faced man pops his head out and says, "Hello old chap, what's the matter with you then?" "Piston broke, I think," says the monk to which the man in the car replies, "Me too, but what's up with the motor?"

****

A man is walking along a remote beach on the south coast of England. After about 20 minutes he hears a deep, booming voice say, "DIG!" He looks up, down, left and right, but he cannot see where the voice could possibly have come from, so he carries on. "I SAID DIG!" says the same deep, booming voice. The man figures that the sensible thing to do under these circumstances is to do as he's told, so he starts digging in the sand at the point where he first heard the voice. After about ten minutes he digs up a little metal box, about one foot square. On the front of it is an old rusted padlock. He hears a deep, booming voice say, "OPEN!" so he pulls and pushes and tweaks and bends until the padlock breaks. Inside, the box is full of gold coins. The deep, booming voice says, "TO THE CASINO!" so the man packs up the box, puts it in his car and drives to the nearest casino. He's had a right result so far, he reckons, so he may as well carry on. He changes the coins for a big stack of chips and starts to wander round the casino when the deep, booming voice says, "ROULETTE!" so he goes to the roulette table. There are a few people playing, but he has no problem getting in on the game. Just then, the deep, booming voice says, "TWENTY-SEVEN" so he puts a couple of chips on that number. "ALL OF IT," the deep, booming voice says so the man loads all the rest of the chips onto number 27. The croupier spins the wheel and rolls the ball. The crowd gathered around the table is silent as the ball spins. And spins. And spins. Eventually, it stops on... number 26. And the deep, booming voice says, "SHIT!"

****

A priest is shopping in the local town when he returns to his car and discovers he has been given a parking ticket. The traffic warden is still writing out the ticket when he arrives. The priest asks, "Oh, you couldn't waive the ticket could you now son?" But the traffic warden replies, "Oh, Father, I'm so sorry, but I've begun to write it and I'm not allowed to stop halfway through. If you'd just been a minute quicker..." "Oh well," says the priest, "I'm terrible with parking, I never remember what the time is or where I've parked, to be sure." "That's very decent of you, Father," says the traffic warden, "quite often when this happens us traffic wardens get given a whole load of abuse." "Oh my goodness, that's awful," says the priest, "after all you're only doing your job aren't you? Now, there's a tea party at the abbey this Sunday, would you like to come over?" "Well, Father, that's very nice of you to ask, I'd love to. And thanks again for being so understanding," says the traffic warden. "And perhaps you'd like to bring your father and your mother, too," says the priest, "I could marry the pair of them while I'm at it!"

****

A man joins an order of silent monks. He doesn't say a word for ten years. After that time, there is a meal held in his honour and the head monk says to him, "Brother Peter, you have been with us for ten years now, you are permitted to break your vow of silence and to say whatever you'd like to say." Brother Peter says, "I'd quite like to have some more food in the evenings please, I've been getting hungry lately." Another ten years pass and another meal is held in Brother Peter's honour. The head monk makes another speech: "Brother Peter, you have been with us for another ten years now, you are permitted to break your vow of silence and to say whatever you'd like to say." Brother Peter says, "I'd quite like to have some more wine in the evenings please, I've been getting thirsty lately." Another ten years pass and another meal is held in Brother Peter's honour. The head monk makes his customary speech: "Brother Peter, you have been with us for another ten years now, you are permitted to break your vow of silence and to say whatever you'd like to say." Brother Peter says, "Father, I think I'm going to leave the order, I don't really think I'm cut out for this life," to which the father replies, "I'm not surprised Brother Peter – you've done nothing but complain since you got here.'

✱✱✱✱

Two nuns are shipped in from Ireland to the United States of America. As they are walking from the docks to the convent they walk past a hot dog stand. "Well would you look at that sister. I did not know that they ate dogs in this country. How weird," said one nun to the other. Her companion replied, "Yes sister, but now that we are to live here, should we not do as the Americans do? I think that we should at least try to eat some dog should we not?" Both of the nuns go over to the vendor and they buy a hot dog each. The vendor hands them each a foil-wrapped "dog". The nuns walk off, unwrapping their food. The first nun stares at hers, and then leans over her friend's shoulder before asking, "Um, so, er, sister, which part of the dog did you get then?"

****

A man is confused about sex and the Sabbath day. He just cannot work out whether having sex on the Sabbath is a sin or not because he doesn't know whether it is work or play. He goes to see his local priest and asks him what his opinion is on this question. The priest gets his Bible down and flicks through it, reading a passage here and a passage there. Eventually he tells the man, "Well my son, after consulting the good book I have decided that sex is closest to work and that therefore you should not practise it on the Sabbath." The man thanks the priest but, as that wasn't really the answer he was looking for, he decides to go and see the local minister, who is married and may see things a bit more his way. He asks the minister the question and, to his disappointment, the minister gives him the same answer as the priest, "No sex on the Sabbath." The man decides to go and see another type of holy man – the local Rabbi. The Rabbi is asked the question and he ponders it over. Eventually he says, "Well my son, I have come to the conclusion that sex is definitely play so therefore you can have sex on the Sabbath." The man says, "That's great Rabbi, but how do you come to that conclusion when so many others disagree?" The Rabbi thinks a little and then says quietly, "If sex were work, my wife would get the maid to do it!"

****

Three Rabbis were playing golf one day. Another fellow, who had no golfing partner, asked if he could join in to make up a foursome. The Rabbis were more than willing and they all had a jolly good round of golf. At the end of the game the man had lost miserably, and his score was a good 30 shots higher than all the Rabbis. He found this confusing, because he's quite a keen weekend golfer, and the Rabbis are men of the cloth. So he asks, "How come you guys are all such good golfers?" One of the Rabbis replies, "Well son, when you lead a good, religious and pure life as part of a temple, your rewards are many. Being good at golf is just one of our rewards." So the man goes home and has a think, and decides, what the hey, I don't have much going on in my life anyway, I may as well go for it and try to improve my golf. So he finds a temple near where he lives, he joins it and attends classes three times a week. One year later the four of them all play golf again, but it is the same story: the man loses miserably again. "So what's that all about?" he asks the Rabbis again. "I joined a temple, I go three times a week and I lead a good, pure life." One of the Rabbis replies, "Which temple did you join?" and the man says, "Shalom Shalom on 4th Avenue." The Rabbi says, "Oh no! That one's for tennis!"

****

A Sloaney Londoner is getting old so she decides to make her will and to include her final requests. She is talking to her priest and she tells him that when she has been cremated she would like to have her remains scattered in Harvey Nics, dear. "But why's that?" asks the priest. The woman replies, "I want to be sure that my daughters will visit me at least once a week!"

****

There are two priests who ride bicycles to their parish church every week. One day one of the priests shows up to "work" without his bicycle. The other priest says to him, "Where has your bike gone Father Michael?" to which Father Michael replies, "I'm not really sure, but I think it's been stolen!" The other priest tells him to read out the ten commandments at the next sermon he gives, and by the time he gets to "Thou Shalt Not Steal", someone will own up to stealing the bicycle from him. The next time the two priests see each other they are both on bicycles again. The other priest asks Father Michael, "So you made the thief own up then did you father?" Father Michael says, "Well not really. I took your advice, sure enough, and I was reading out the Ten Commandments. I got to 'Thou Shalt Not Commit Adultery', when I all of a sudden remembered where I'd left my bike!"

****

A drunk staggers into church and manages to make his way into one of the confessionals. He sits there in silence. The priest coughs once to get the man's attention, but the man just ignores him and sits there. The priest can see that the man isn't asleep so he coughs again, only this time louder. The man still ignores him. The priest then knocks on the divider in a last attempt to get the man to speak. This seems to have the desired effect, and the man shouts to the priest, "It's no use knocking, there's no paper in this bloody one either!"

****

A woman goes to see her priest because she has a problem with the couple of female parrots that she owns – they just will not behave themselves. All they can say is, "Hello, we are prostitutes. Do you wanna have a good time?" The father agrees that that's a terrible situation, but he realizes very quickly that he, himself can provide a simple solution. He asks the woman to bring her two parrots over to his house, because he too has two parrots – his are male – and he has bought them up to read the Bible and to pray and all that sort of "good" stuff. He figures that his good parrots will be a very good influence on her "bad" parrots and that all will live happily together eventually. The next day, the woman brings her two female parrots over to the priest's house. She sees the priest's two parrots in their cage. They are praying, burning incense and fiddling with their rosary beads, all in a very devout manner. The woman puts her parrots down next to the priest's parrots and hers pipe up, "Hello, we are prostitutes. Do you wanna have a good time?" Upon hearing this, one of the priest's parrots turns to the other one and says, "Put the good book away my man, our prayers have been answered!'

****

A man goes to confession. In the booth he says, "Forgive me, Father, for I have sinned. I... almost... had an affair with a woman." "Almost? What do you mean almost?" says the priest, not really understanding what the man is going on about. "Well, Father," the man continues, "we got undressed and rubbed against one another, but then we both thought better of it and so we stopped." "Very good," says the priest, "but rubbing up against it is just the same as putting it in. You must not go near that woman again. You must say five Hail Marys and you must put €50 in the donation box by the door." The man thanks the priest and walks to the door of the church. He stops by the donation box, pauses and then starts to leave. The priest runs up to him and says, "Oi, I saw that, you didn't put anything in the donation box did you?" "Well no, I didn't father," the man says, "I rubbed up against it, and as you say, that's the same as putting it in!"

****

A priest and a nun were travelling through the desert on a camel. It was a very long, hot journey and the camel became ill and died, leaving the two of them stranded in the middle of the hot desert. After a couple of days, the pair of them are resigned to their fate and discuss all sorts of things, including sex. The priest is talking about how he's never had sex with a woman, so he pulls out his knob and says to the nun, "This is my life-giving tool." The nun, ever hopeful, says, "Oh, really? So why don't you stick it in the camel and give us the chance of getting the hell out of here?"

****

Ex-President Bill Clinton dies and goes to Hell. Satan, who's been waiting for him at the gate, greets him warmly. Now it turns out that Hell is a bit full at the moment, so Bill will be replacing some lucky person, who will get to go up to "the other place" instead. The good news for Bill is that he gets to choose who he can replace. Satan tells Bill to follow him as he leads him to three doorways. Satan opens the first door and Bill sees a man chained to the wall, smashing big rocks into smaller ones with a big hammer. At the sight of this, Bill goes pale and says, "Oh, no, I couldn't handle that: no way." Satan opens the second door and Bill sees a man up to his neck in mud, just able to breathe and keep his head above water. At the sight of this, Bill goes even paler, and says, "Oh, no, I couldn't handle that, no way." Satan opens the third door and Bill sees a man tied to a pole, totally naked. Kneeling in front of him is Monica Lewinsky, giving him a blowjob. At the sight of this, Bill gets a bit of colour back in his cheeks. "Well, I think I could handle this," he says. "Great choice," says the Devil. "Monica – you can go now."

✳✳✳✳

An Amish boy and his father decided to visit a shopping mall. They were amazed by everything they saw, but especially by two shiny, silver walls that moved magically forward and backwards together by themselves. The young boy said to his father, "Daddy, what is this for? What miracle is this?" and the father replied that he did not know. As the two watched, an 80-year-old lady walked in and the doors closed. Lights above the doors flashed upwards and then down again, before the doors opened again, silently, and a beautiful 25-year-old woman walked out. The father and son looked at each other before the father said to the boy, "Go and get your mother!"

✳✳✳✳

A little boy is sitting with his mother at a service when the sermon is about to start. He turns to her and says, "Mummy, I don't feel well. I think I am going to be sick." The mother is rather embarrassed, but it appears the rest of the congregation hadn't heard him. "You can't be sick here," she tells him. "I tell you what, go out now, before the sermon starts, and if you have to be sick, then at least you won't disrupt the priest or the service." The boy disappears and when the sermon ends, he makes his way back and sits down next to his mother. "Well, were you sick?" she asks felicitously. "Yes, Mummy, I was and I feel much better now." "Good, I am pleased you were so quiet. But, tell me, where were you sick?" she asks, thinking about the mess she would have to clear up. "I knew exactly where to go," he said proudly. "There was a big box at the back of the church with 'For the sick' written on it."

✳✳✳✳

Boys & Girls

10

Jokes about the
birds and the bees

Little Johnny's dad picks him up after school because Johnny has been trying out for a part in the school play. Johnny is all excited and his dad says, "So, son, it looks like you got a part – that's great!" Johnny says, "Yes, dad, I did: I get to play the part of a man who's been married for a quarter of a century." "That's great, son," says his father, "and if you keep trying harder and harder, one day you'll get a speaking part!"

****

Jake moves to Australia after working all his life in the City. He buys a farm in the remotest part of the outback he can find. His post arrives once a week, his groceries once a month and he can call the flying doctor on his radio if he has an emergency. One night, after six months of this, Jake is finishing his dinner when he hears a knock on the door. He walks up, opens it and sees a huge outbacker standing in front of him. "G'day, mate," says the outbacker. "I'm your nearest neighbour, Bruce Sheldon, from 20 miles east. I'm having a party Saturday night and I thought you might like to come along, mate." "That'd be great," says Jake. "I haven't really spoken to anyone for six months. Thanks a lot." Bruce is about to turn away, but instead says, "I think I'd better warn you, though: there'll be some serious drinking going on." "Not a problem," says Jake, "I like a couple of pints myself." Bruce is about to turn away again, but instead says, "Better warn you though, there'll probably be some fighting, too." "Not a problem," says Jake, "I know how to keep out of trouble." Bruce is about to turn away again, but instead says, "Better warn you though, there'll probably be some pretty wild sex, too." "Not a problem," says Jake, "I've been alone for six months, remember. Now, what time should I show up?" Bruce turns once more and says, "Whenever you like, mate: there's only going to be me and you there anyway!'

****

A man and woman have been married for what seems like forever. They have eight grown-up children and countless grandchildren. On their 60th wedding anniversary they have a very candid conversation. The wife says to her husband, "Honey, since we are so old now and we've been together for so long, I'm going to be totally honest with you. Is there anything you'd like to know about me and our relationship over the past six decades that you'd like to ask me about? If there is, I promise that I will answer you with total honesty." The husband pauses for a while, and then says, "Dear, this isn't easy for me to say, but there is actually something that has been eating away at me for quite a few years now. It's just that of all our kids, there's one who looks decidedly different from the others. You know the one I mean, I'm sure, and I'm sure it's nothing but, as I say, I've wondered about this for years and I would like to know if he had a different father from the rest of the kids." The wife looks down at her feet and sighs loudly. "Well, dear, I'm sorry to say it, but you're right. I cannot tell a lie: that child did indeed have a different father from all the others." The husband looks miserable, but he's still curious. "And who would that be?" he asks. "Well, dear…" begins the wife slowly, "…you."

****

At the National Improvized Poetry Competition, there were two finalists. One was an Oxford graduate, the other a dustbin man from Suffolk. As a tiebreak they had two minutes to make up a poem containing the word "Timbuktu". The Oxford graduate read his poem first:

> We came across the desert,
> Miles across the sand,
> Both on camels, me and you,
> On our search for Timbuktu.

The audience cheered and thought the bumpkin would have no chance against so eloquent an effort. However, the dustbin man won hands-down with his effort:

> Me and Tim a-huntin' went
> Met three birds in a field in Kent
> They were three and us but two
> So I bucked one and Timbuktu!

****

A young mother teaches her son to go to the bathroom by numbers. She teaches him the following lesson: 1. Unzip your flies. 2. Gently lift out your family jewels. 3. Pull back the foreskin. 4. Let nature take its course. 5. Slide the foreskin forward. 6. Replace the family jewels. 7. Zip back up. The mother would often check that he was following instructions by listening outside the door of the bathroom. She would hear, "One, two, three, four, five, six, seven. All done!" However, one day she was walking past the bathroom and was disturbed to hear, "Three–five, three–five, three–five, three–five…"

****

A farmer is having trouble with his prize stud bull, which has a herd of 300 cows to sort out. It won't do what is required of it, so the farmer takes it to the vet. Without even examining the animal, the vet hands the farmer a small bottle of pills and says, "Grind one of these into its feed, stand back and watch it go!" Two weeks later, the farmer returns to the vet and says, "Veterinary, that was truly incredible. I did what you said and as soon as he'd eaten the feed he leaped over the fence and screwed all 300 cows in less than an hour!" The vet says, "So what's the problem then – why are you back?" The farmer says, "Well, I was wondering: it's a bit personal, but I've got a hot date with a 21-year-old tonight and I could really do with one of those tablets. I'm not really the man I used to be, after all." "Well, I can't really let you have a whole one," says the vet, "but I guess a quarter of a pill wouldn't do much harm!" So he gives a quarter-pill to the farmer, who goes off to prepare for his date. A few days later, the farmer is back at the vet's again. "What is it this time?" asks the vet. "Well, the pill worked fine – 40 times that one night," says the farmer. "So what's up, then?" asks the vet. "Well, now I need something for my wrist," says the farmer. "She never showed up!"

****

It was the night before Christmas and a rather lonely lady, who hadn't got laid in a very long time, was waiting for Father Christmas to come down the chimney at her house. When he did, she removed her shirt and said, "Oh, Santa, please stay a while." Santa said, "Ho ho ho, lady: I'd love to, but I've got toys to deliver to children around the world." So she dropped her skirt and says, "Oh Santa, please stay a while." Santa says, "Ho ho ho, lady, I'd love to, but I've got toys to deliver to children around the world." So she stripped naked and said, "Oh, Santa, please stay a while." So Santa said, "Well, I'm never going to get up the chimney with my dick in this state, so I guess I'd better stay a while!"

****

A guy walks into a gun shop. "I'd like to buy a laser sight for a rifle, please." The salesman fetches one and encourages him to try it out. The man is looking around the neighbourhood when he sees, through a window, a man and a woman on the job. "Whoa! Check this out!" he says to the salesman, who has a look for himself. His eyes nearly jump out of his head as he sees that it is his wife with another man. No decent shot himself, he makes the guy the following offer: "If you can shoot him in the dick and her in the head I'll give you the laser sight and the rifle of your choice." "Sure thing," says the guy, and he takes aim and looses off a shot. "What luck – two for one: job done," he says.

****

A man is out shopping one Saturday when he finds a new brand of condom. He is impressed by the brand: "Olympic Condoms – for winners." When he gets home he shows his wife, who asks him, "What's so special about Olympic, then?" "That's the cool thing," he says. "They come in three colours: gold, silver and bronze." "And which colour will you be wearing tonight?" the wife questions. "Well, gold, of course, darling," the man replies. Quick as a flash, the wife quips, "Why don't you try silver? It'd be nice if you came second for a change!"

****

A mother walked into the bathroom one day and was shocked to find her son scrubbing away furiously at his cock using a toothbrush and toothpaste. "Oh, my God: what on earth's going on?" she said. "Don't try and stop me, Mum," the boy said. "I'm doing this three times a day because if you think I'm going to end up with a cavity that looks as bad as my sister's you've got another think coming!"

****

One morning the farmer's son got up early to go and play on the farm, but his mother told him he would have to do chores because now he was old enough to be helping out. The boy didn't like the thought of this much, but didn't have a lot of choice. He started in the barn, where he milked the cow. When he'd finished he booted the cow up the arse. Then he went to feed the pig. When he'd finished, he booted the pig up the arse. The he went to feed the chickens. When he'd finished, he booted the chickens up the arse. Now his chores were done, he went back to the house for breakfast. His mother gave him a bowl of dry cornflakes. "What about milk and my fried breakfast?" asked the boy. "Well, you don't get any milk because you kicked the cow up the arse," said his mother. "And you don't get any bacon because you kicked the pig up the arse," she continued, "and you don't get any eggs because you kicked the chickens up the arse." At that moment, the farmer walks in as the cat walks past the door. In a bad mood, the farmer launches a kick at the cat and gets it up the arse. The boy is silent for a while, then looks at his mother and says, "Do you want to give him the bad news or shall I?"

****

A robber escapes from prison and breaks into a house occupied by a young couple. He ties them up and leaves them alone in the bedroom for a while. As soon as they are alone, the husband turns to his young wife, skimpily dressed in her black nightie, and says, "Now listen, dear. This man probably hasn't had sex with a woman for years. If he wants to have sex, just go along with it and pretend that you're enjoying it. It will probably mean the difference between living and dying for us." "I'm so glad you feel that way, my darling," said the wife, "because he just told me he loves your smooth skin and firm arse!"

****

A drunken bum is sitting on a bar stool when a really high-class bird sits down next to him. He immediately turns around and says to her, "Hey, darlin'. How's about you and me getting together for a bit of how's your father? I've got a couple of Euro and you look like you could do with a little cash!" The woman looks at him coldly before replying, "What makes you think I charge by the inch?'

****

Janine had been married to Tim for 75 years. When he passed on she just couldn't envisage life without him, so she decided to end it all by herself. Remembering that Tim had an old army pistol and some live ammunition, Janine did some research. She found out on the Internet that a shot to the heart would be the best way to get it over with quickly. She read a page that said her heart would be a couple of inches below the left breast. She said her last rites, turned off the gas, cancelled the milk and pulled the trigger. Later that night Janine was admitted to the local hospital with a bullet wound to the left thigh.

****

A young secondary school teacher is informed that, due to cutbacks, she will have to give her class their sex education lessons herself. Not wanting to have to explain much or draw pictures, she decides to use a mathematical approach and gets some flashcards for the following day's lessons. At the start of the lesson she holds up the first card, a picture of a breast, and says to the class, "Does anyone know what this is?" Susan puts up her hand and says, "I know; I know. It's a breast, and my Mummy has two of them." "That's very good, Susan," says the teacher and holds up the next card. It's of a penis. "Does anyone know what this is?" she asks. Tim puts his hand up and says, "I know; I know. It's a penis, and my Daddy has two of them." "Well, that's very good, Tim: it is a penis, but your Daddy can't have two of them." Tim replies, "He does, miss. He's got a little one he pees with and a great big one he brushes Mummy's teeth with!"

****

Christopher invites his nosy mother over for dinner. She's been encouraging him to find a wife for years, and when she arrives she notices that the live-in housekeeper is a very attractive woman who gets on very well with her son. She can't help wondering if maybe there's something going on – they get on so well – but her son denies everything: "Mother, I assure you that my relationship with my housekeeper is strictly professional." A few days later, the housekeeper tells Christopher that ever since his mother came over for dinner she has been unable to find the silver tray that the brandy is always served on. A curious affair indeed, thinks Christopher: I wonder what my mother is up to now. So he writes his mother a letter:

Dear Mother,
Regarding my silver tray. I'm obviously not saying that you did take it, and I'm not saying that you did not take it, but the fact remains that I have been unable to find it since you came over for dinner.
Love, Christopher.

A couple of days later, Christopher receives a reply:

Dear Christopher,
Regarding your housekeeper. I'm obviously not saying that you do sleep with her, and I'm not saying that you do not sleep with her, but the fact remains that if she was sleeping in her own bed she would have found the silver tray by now!
Love, Mother.

****

A man and woman are sitting next to each other in the first-class compartment of an aeroplane. Suddenly the man sneezes, but instead of wiping his nose, he pulls out his penis and wipes the tip with a handkerchief. The woman cannot believe it and thinks she must be imagining things. A couple of minutes go by and the man sneezes again. It's the same story – he pulls his penis out and wipes it with a handkerchief. The woman is absolutely astonished and stares at the man, who doesn't seem to notice. Five minutes later the man sneezes again. He goes through the same process and this time the woman can bear it no longer. She turns to him and says, as calmly as she possibly can, "That's three times you have sneezed, and three times you have wiped your penis on a handkerchief. It's absolutely disgusting! What kind of sick, twisted individual are you?" The man replies, "Goodness. I'm so sorry that I offended you, but I suffer from a very rare condition which means every time I sneeze I have an orgasm." The woman feels slightly guilty and replies, "Oh, I'm sorry: I should have realized. You poor thing. What on earth do you take for it?" The man turns around, looks her square in the face and says, "Pepper."

****

A young wife was frustrated by the lack of spice in her and her husband's sex life, so she decided to see what she could do about it. Straight after work she went shopping and bought herself a pair of crotchless panties in a sex shop. She ran home and put on her new panties, along with a particularly short skirt. When her husband came home from work she fixed him a drink and sat across from him as he drank it. "Now you've had some of that, sugar..." she cooed as she slowly spread her legs, "...perhaps you'd like some of this?" "God, no!" screamed the husband. "Look what it's done to your underwear!"

****

One Sunday, a man is working in the garden as his wife gets up and bathes. He is clearing leaves and soon realizes that he cannot find his rake, the essential tool for the job. He can see his wife in their bedroom window, so he shouts up, "Where's my rake?" The wife doesn't understand him and mouths, "What?" Again the man shouts, "Where's my rake?" The wife still doesn't understand, so shrugs her shoulders to signify a lack of comprehension. The man, tiring of shouting, points to his eye, then his knee, and then makes a raking motion with both hands. The wife is still clueless, so shrugs again, to say, "What?" The man repeats the gestures, and mouths "eye, knee, the rake" as he does so. The wife understands finally, and signals her reply. She points to her eye, her left breast, her arse and finally her crotch. The man's eyes nearly pop out and it is obvious he hasn't got a clue what she is going on about. Giving up, he walks into the house and runs upstairs. "What the hell was that all about?" he says. The wife replies, "Eye, left tit, behind, the bush!"

****

Why are Monica Lewinsky's cheeks so puffed up?
She's withholding evidence.

What did Bill Clinton say to Monica Lewinsky?
"I didn't, 'say wreck my election,' I said …".

****

One day in a jewellery shop a man is in the process of buying a really expensive necklace with a lovely silver locket on it. The jeweller asks him, "Would you like her name engraved on it?" The man has a think and then replies, "No: just put 'To my one and only love.' That way, if we split up and she throws it back in anger, I'll be able to recycle!'

****

A man gets himself an Audi TT with a share bonus windfall at work and takes Friday night to drive it around the M25. As he gets more used to the car he starts to go faster and faster. Eventually he winds up at over 100 miles per hour. Just as the needle goes over the hundred, he sees flashing lights in his rearview mirror and he pulls over. The policeman walks up to his window, leans in and says, "Look here mate, I've had a rough day, I'm nearly off, so if you can give me an excuse I've never heard before I'll let you off the ticket, the fine and the driving ban." The man can't believe his potential luck and excitedly says, "Well officer, my wife ran away with a policeman last week and I was driving so quickly away from you 'cos I thought you were trying to give her back!" "You take it easy sir, and have a good weekend," said the policeman as he turned to go back to his car.

****

An old guy begins to feel his age, and at 50 decides to treat himself to a facelift. When it's done, he feels really good – years younger. On his way back from the surgery he stops off at a newsagent to get the paper. He chats to the shopkeeper, and eventually says, "I hope you don't mind me asking, but how old do you reckon I am?" "No problem," says the shopkeeper, "about 35?" "It's my 50th birthday!" says the man, overjoyed. Next, he goes to get some fish and chips. He chats to the assistant and eventually says, "I hope you don't mind me asking, but how old do you reckon I am?" "No problem," says the chipper, "about 32?" "It's my 50th birthday!" says the man, overjoyed again. The man decides to get a taxi home, and stands in the queue to get one. Behind him is an old lady and they get talking. The man says to her, "I hope you don't mind me asking, but how old do you reckon I am?" "No problem," says the old lady, "but I'm 85 and my eyesight's not so good. If I put my hand down your trousers and play with your balls for a couple of minutes I'll be able to tell exactly how old you are." This came as a bit of a shock to the man, but he figured what the hell, and let the old lady put her hand down his trousers. After a couple of minutes the old lady says, "It's your 50th birthday." The man is amazed. "That's incredible," he says. "How on earth did you know that?" The old lady replies, "I was standing behind you in the fish and chip shop!'

****

There once was a beautiful young woman who wanted to use her good looks to get rich quick. So she started to hang around older men in the hope of netting one for herself to marry and to shag them to death on their wedding night. She pretty quickly found herself a rich 80-year-old who looked frail, and their romance went quickly and effectively. Three months later it was their wedding day. All went well and in the evening they found themselves in a five-star hotel in Paris. They both retired to their separate bathrooms and she emerged first, seductively dressed as she slipped between the satin sheets of the huge bed they were to share. The man's bathroom door opens and he walked out sporting a condom over a 12-inch erection. He was carrying a pair of earplugs and some nose plugs, too. The woman's heart sank and she began to suspect something was up. Tentatively, she asked, "Er... what are those for, dear?" The old man replies, "These take care of the two things I can't stand the most: the sound of women screaming and the smell of burning rubber!'

****

A masked man runs through the door of a sperm bank. He is brandishing a shotgun. He leaps over the counter and points the gun at the receptionist. "Open the safe!" he barks at her. "What?" she says. "There's no money here: we're a sperm bank, not a money bank." "Just do it!" the guy continues. "Just open the goddamned safe and don't talk back. Don't make me hurt you, lady." So the lady leads him out back and opens the safe. It is just a big refrigerator full of sperm samples. "Now take a sample out," the guy snaps. The woman obliges. "Now, drink it," the guy says. "But it's sperm," the woman says. "Don't make me mad – just do it!" shouts the man. Fearing the worst, the woman pops the cap off the bottle and drinks the sperm. She chokes a couple of times but drains the bottle. "Another one," says the guy. She takes another bottle from the racks and drinks it. At that moment the man drops his gun and pulls off his mask. The woman cannot believe her eyes – the man who just had a gun at her head is her husband! "You see," he shouts at her, "it wasn't that bloody difficult, was it?"

****

A top executive lawyer decides that he needs some holiday and to improve his golf, so combines the two with a week's-worth of golf at his local course. On the first round of the first day, he is playing behind a woman whom the lawyer notices is very attractive – and not bad at golf, either. He makes the effort and catches up with her quite quickly. He suggests to her that they play together and she agrees. They begin to play and it soon turns out that they are very evenly matched. Eventually the woman wins with the last stroke on the last hole. They have got on really well, so the man offers his congratulations and offers the woman a lift home. As they are driving, the woman tells the man how much fun she's had, and that she is surprised at how well they got on and how close the competition was. They stop at her place, and she says, "I'd like to show you just how much I appreciated the game and your company," she says, and proceeds to give the lawyer a blowjob. The next morning the lawyer sees the woman teeing off at the first and again suggests a partnership. She agrees, and they play another round of close, competitive golf. The man is pretty disappointed that he didn't manage to win the previous day's game so he really puts everything into it, but it is to no avail. The lady wins once more, again by just one stroke. Again, he gives her a lift home and she gives him a blowjob. This pattern carries on all week, with the woman winning the golf every day. The man is pretty sick about this, but he's getting to spend a lot of time with a beautiful woman who performs sexual favours for him, too, so he's not really complaining. On the Friday night as he is driving her home, he announces that in honour of spending such a great time with her, he's booked them a table for a candlelit dinner at the most exclusive restaurant in town, and then a penthouse appartment at the best hotel. Upon hearing this, the woman bursts into tears, sobbing, "I can't; I can't." The lawyer asks her what on earth is wrong. She sobs out that she just can't go with him, not because she doesn't want to, but because she isn't really a woman – she is, in fact, a transvestite. The guy is gobsmacked and says nothing. "I'm so sorry," she cries. "You total bastard!" he screams suddenly, all red in the face, "You bloody cheat. You've been playing off women's tees all week!"

****

There was a farmer with three daughters. One Saturday night they each had a date. One by one the dates arrived and the farmer answered the door each time. The first fellow knocked on the door. The farmer answered and the fellow said, "Hello, Mr Farmer. My name is Joe, I'm here to take your daughter Flo out to eat some dough." "That's just fine," said the farmer, and off went Joe with the eldest daughter. The second fellow knocked on the door. The farmer answered and the fellow said, "Hello, Mr Farmer. My name is Freddy, I'm here to take your daughter Betty out to eat spaghetti." "That's just fine," said the farmer and off went Freddy with the middle daughter. The third fellow knocked on the door. The farmer answered and the fellow said, "Hello, Mr Farmer. My name is Chuck –" "Get the hell out of my house," yelled the farmer.

****

A man is drinking in his local watering-hole in New York when he spots a bit of top totty hanging out with a really cheap, loser type. He's amazed that a dullard like that can pull such top crumpet, so he goes up to the bartender and asks him about it. He discovers that the woman is a prostitute, so he keeps an eye on her and, sure enough, a while later, she leaves on the man's arm and comes back later with someone else. The next night the man is in the same bar and in comes the prostitute. He still thinks she looks magnificent, so he goes up to her and asks her what her rates are. She is totally unfazed, and says, "Well, my rates start at $100 for a handjob and go up from there." "A hundred dollars," the guy interrupts, "for a handjob? You must be joking!" "Listen, buddy," says the woman, pointing out of the window at a huge Mercedes outside, "I bought that car for cash with the money I made from giving handjobs! Trust me: it'll be worth it." The man is certainly impressed, and thinks for a few seconds before deciding to get himself a handjob from the woman. They leave together and the man gets what he thinks is probably the finest sexual experience that he's ever had with anyone. The next night he is back in the bar, eagerly awaiting the woman. When she shows up, he walks straight up to her, saying, "Last night really was incredible." "Of course it was: I told you, didn't I?" the prostitute replies, "but just you wait until you try one of my blowjobs." The man is tempted, but he asks, "and how much would that be?" The woman replies, "$1,000." "One thousand dollars?" the guy almost shouts, before the woman says, "Listen, buddy: I bought myself a ten-storey downtown condominium for cash with the money I made from giving blowjobs. Trust me: it'll be worth it." The man is impressed again and, based on the evidence of the previous evening, decides to get himself a blowjob from the woman. They leave together and the man gets what he knows is far and away the greatest single experience of his life – he nearly faints! The next night he is back in the bar, waiting again. He is so excited he can hardly sit in a chair. When the prostitute does eventually show up, he runs up to her and says, "You're the best: you're the best: just tell me what it'll cost for some pussy!" The woman grabs his hand and pulls him outside the bar into the street. Away in the distance he can see Manhattan. She says, "You see that island?" To which the guy replies, "Come on – you can't be serious!" The prostitute nods her head and says, "Yup: if I had a pussy, I'd own Manhattan!"

****

An Italian, a Frenchman and a Texan were talking about making love to their partners. The Italian began, "Last-a night, I make the love to my-a wife three times. She have three times joy. She was hin ecstasy this-a morning." The Frenchman continued, "I made lurve to mah wife seeks times last night. Zis morning she make me ze omelette and she say to me zat she could never lurve anozzer man een er life!" The Texan doesn't say a word, so the Frenchman said to him, "And ow many times did you make ze love wis your wife last night?" "Just the once," the Texan replied. "Only once!" snorted the Italian, "and what did your poor wife-a say to you this morning?" "Don't stop," drawled the Texan.

****

A man had a beautiful but very demanding wife. She always wanted the latest fashion clothes and beautiful jewellery, but he didn't really make enough money to get her all that she wanted. One day she comes home showing off a brand-new diamond necklace. "Wow," he says to her, "where did you get that?" "Oh, I won it at bingo, darling," she says, rather unconvincingly. The next day the wife comes home wearing a brand-new mink coat. "Wow," he says to her, "where did you get that?" "Oh, I won it at bingo, darling – I've had a lucky week, you know." The next day the wife comes home in a brand-new Porsche. "Wow," he says, "where did you get that?" "Oh, stop asking me all those awkward questions, please. Leave me alone and do something useful. Go upstairs and run me a bath, there's a dear." The wife comes upstairs and into the bathroom. There's only a tiny amount of water in the bottom of the bath. The wife says, "What's up with the depth of that bath? That's not even going to reach my pussy!" And the husband replies, "Didn't want to get your bingo card wet, dear!'

****

A man dies while having sex but his erection stays hard. At the funeral parlour they discuss the situation with his wife and she gives them permission to cut it off in order to get the lid on the coffin. The wife keeps the penis, and later that night steals back and shoves it up the dead man's rear end. The next day, at the funeral, she peers over the coffin and, noticing a tear in the dead man's eye, whispers, "I told you it hurt, you heartless bastard!"

****

An old soak is looking for a whorehouse and stumbles into a chiropodist's office. He walks up to the front desk and is directed to one of the inspection rooms. Without looking up, the receptionist waves him over to the inspection table and without looking up says, "Stick it through the curtain." Thinking, "How cool is this?', the drunk pulls his plonker out and sticks it through the middle of the curtain. "That's not a foot!" screams the doctor on the other side. "Well, lah-di-dah," says the drunk, "I didn't know there was a minimum!'

✶✶✶✶

A woman is tidying up around the house one day when she hears a strange humming noise coming from her daughter's bedroom. The mother knocks on the door but just opens it immediately. She walks in and finds her daughter lying naked on the bed, pleasuring herself with a vibrator. The mother is a little shocked, but retains her composure and says, "What on earth are you doing that for, dear?" The daughter replies, "Well, mother, I am nearly 40 years old and I live at home with my parents. I never date guys, so I figure this is the nearest thing I'll get to a husband!" That night her father can't sleep, so he wanders downstairs and hears a strange humming noise coming from the front room. He walks in and finds his daughter lying naked on the sofa, pleasuring herself with a vibrator. The father is a little shocked, but retains his composure and says, "What on earth are you doing that for, dear?" The daughter replies, "Well, father, I am nearly 40 years old and I live at home with my parents. I never date guys, so I figure this is the nearest thing I'll get to a husband!" The next day the mother is once more tidying up around the house when she hears that same humming noise coming from the front room. She walks in and, to her surprise, she sees her husband watching TV with the vibrator just placed on the sofa beside him. "What the hell are you doing?" she says to her husband, shocked. He replies, "Just watching the game with the son-in-law."

****

A well-to-do woman visits her doctor, saying, "Doc, my problem is a bit embarrassing and I'm going to have to show you rather than explain it." "That's fine," says the doc, used to such things, "just show me where the problem is." The woman lifts up her skirt and opens her legs. There, right at the top of each thigh, on the inside of each leg, are large, green circles. "Do you know what it is doc? It's been troubling me for weeks now and I've no idea what the cause could be." The doctor drops to his knees and spends some time examining the area that has turned green. After a while he says, "I've never seen anything like it, unless…" "Yes, doctor?" says the woman expectantly. "Unless – let me think – have you been seeing someone who wears large earrings lately?" The woman is somewhat surprised but says, "Well, yes, doc; I have, as a matter of fact. But why do you ask?" "Well, perhaps you should tell them that their earrings aren't real gold!"

****

After his first day at school, Timmy comes home full of questions for his parents. Unfortunately, some of them are not really what his parents hoped he'd be learning at school. So Timmy goes up to his mother and says, "Mummy, what's a pussy? Everyone says that word in the playground and I don't know what it means." Timmy's mother picks up an illustrated dictionary and flicks to the page with a cat on it. She shows him the picture. Then Timmy says, "Mummy, what's a bitch? Everyone says that word in the playground and I don't know what it means." Timmy's mother picks up the dictionary and flicks to the page with a dog on it, and shows Timmy the female. Timmy is still curious so he goes to find his father. He says, "Daddy, what's a pussy? Everyone says that word in the playground and I'm still not sure what it means." Timmy's dad figures it is time to teach the boy a thing or two, so he picks up a jazzmag, draws a circle around the pussy that's on the page and shows the picture to the boy. "That's a pussy," he says. Then Timmy says, "Daddy, what's a bitch? Everyone says that word in the playground and I'm still not sure what it means." Timmy's father replies, "Everything outside the circle!"

****

In the distant future, a couple of humans land on a distant planet in their spaceship. They are greeted by a couple of natives of the planet, who look remarkably human and who speak the same language. They talk for hours, comparing everything on Earth and on the alien planet. Things are a lot closer than they would have all imagined and the aliens have computers, cars, television, guns and all the other things we have that make life great. Eventually the couples get on to social interaction and, in particuar, how they have sex on their respective planets. It turns out that the aliens have sex pretty much the same way that Earth people do, so the two men suggest that, in order to see the differences, the couples should swap partners and see how things are done on the other planets. The women both agree to this and they all retire for the night. The Earth woman is in the bedroom with the alien man and they both undress. She is a little worried because the alien's member is tiny: a couple of centimetres long and only about a centimetre thick, even when it's hard. "This isn't going to be easy," she says. "What's up?" says the alien, "the size bother you? Not a problem." And he slaps himself on the forehead. As he does so, his member grows longer. He continues to slap and with each hit he gets bigger until he is very impressive-looking. "That's pretty good," says the Earth woman, "but it could do with being a bit thicker." "Not a problem," says the alien again and he begins pulling his ears. With each pull, his member increases in thickness until it is even more impressive. "Amazing!" exclaims the Earth woman, and they shag wildly all night. The next day she meets her husband at breakfast. "How was it for you?" he asks her. "Well, I must admit, they've got some pretty exciting stuff over us," she replies, "but how was it for you?" "Well, I must admit I was a bit disappointed," he says, "I just got a headache. She kept slapping my forehead and pulling my ears all night!'

****

A little boy comes home early from school one day and catches his parents having sex. In fact, the wife is giving the husband a blowjob. The boy asks, "Mummy and Daddy, what are you doing?" so the parents reply, "Making fish sticks," because they figure he's only young and he's never going to know what they're up to, and what does he care anyway? A couple of nights later the boy walks in on them again and as they turn around he says, "Are you making fish sticks again?" Both parents say "Yes". So the boy says, "Well. Mummy, you've got some tartare sauce stuck on your lip!"

★★★★

A little old lady lives in a nursing home. She's losing her marbles and one day she walks up to one of the male patients and lifts up her skirt. She points down and says, "Super pussy," then drops her skirt and walks away. She walks up to another male patient and lifts up her skirt. She points down and says, "Super pussy," then drops her skirt and walks away. Then she walks up to a third male patient and lifts up her skirt. She points down and says "Super pussy" once more. The man looks up at her and says, "I think I'll take the soup, thanks!"

★★★★

A couple have been married for years and years. On their 60th anniversary they decide to go on a second honeymoon. "Let's go to all the same places that we did just after our wedding," the wife says. "Sure," says the husband. "And let's do all the same things that we did just after our wedding," the wife says. "Sure," says the husband. "And we'll make love just like we did after our wedding," the wife says. "Sure," says the husband, "only this time it's me who gets to sit on the side of the bed crying, 'It's too big, it's too big!'"

★★★★

A young newly-wed couple decide to have a romantic weekend away in the mountains in the winter: candlelit dinners, roaring fires and peace and quiet. They arrive in their winter cabin and the husband goes out to chop wood as the wife prepares their lunch. After a while he returns, saying, "Wow! It sure is cold. My hands are freezing." "Well', his wife tells him, "pop them between my thighs, baby: it's pretty hot down there, and sure to warm them up." He does so. After lunch he realizes they are low on wood again, so the husband goes out to chop some more. After a while he returns, saying, "Wow! It sure is cold. My hands are freezing." "Well," his wife tells him, "pop them between my thighs, baby: it's pretty hot down there, and sure to warm them up." He does so again. Later in the evening the husband goes out to chop wood again. After a while he returns, saying, "Wow! It sure is cold. My hands are freezing." But this time the wife says, "For goodness' sake! Don't you ever get cold ears?"

****

A woman and a man are involved in a really nasty car accident. Both their cars are totally demolished, but neither of them are hurt. After they crawl out of their cars, the woman says, "So you're a man – that's interesting. I'm a woman. Wow, just look at our cars! There's nothing left, but we're unhurt. This must be a sign from God that we should meet, get aquainted and live together in peace for the rest of our days." The man feels great at having such good luck, so says, "Oh, yes; I agree with you completely! This must be a sign from the Lord!" The woman continues, "And look at this – another miracle. My car is demolished, but this bottle of wine didn't break. Surely God wants us to drink this wine and celebrate our good fortune." She hands the bottle to the man, who nods his head in agreement, opens the bottle and drinks half of it before handing it back to the woman. The woman takes the bottle and immediately puts the cap back on. The man asks, "Aren't you having any?" The woman replies, "No. I think I'll just wait for the police!" The moral of this story: Women are clever. Don't mess with them.

****

It is Christmas, and a little boy is taken to the local Santa's Grotto to meet the big man himself. Santa picks the boy up, places him on his knee and begins to ask him about what he wants for Christmas. The boy says he doesn't really know what he'd like for Christmas, so Santa makes some suggestions, spelling the words out as he does so, and prodding the boy's nose, so the boy can surely understand. Santa asks him if he'd like a B-I-K-E or a T-R-A-I-N and so on, but the little boy doesn't seem to want any of the "normal" Christmas stuff. So Santa eventually says, "Come on, kid: what do you want for Christmas?" The little boy replies, "I want some P-U-S-S-Y and I know you've got some because I can smell it on your finger!"

****

One day, a sweet little girl goes home to find that her dog has died. He is lying on the lawn on his back with his poor little legs sticking straight up in the air. She quickly runs to her father and asks him why her dog is lying down with his poor little legs in the air. "Well," her father explains, "that's because Jesus will be coming down to help poor doggy up to Heaven, and if his legs are up in the air like that it'll be a whole lot easier for him to go." The very next day when the father comes home, the sweet little girl runs up to him in a dreadful state. "Daddy! Daddy! Mummy almost died today – I'm sure of it!" "Oh, my!" says the father. "How do you know – is she OK?" "Yes, Daddy," the girl says, "she's OK now, but earlier on Mummy's legs were up in the air and she was shouting 'Oh Jesus, I'm coming, I'm coming' and if the postman hadn't been there to hold her down I think she'd be in Heaven now!"

****

A hippy, long-haired youth was on a hitch-hiking holiday through the southern states. In Georgia he got a ride from a really nasty-looking trucker in a check shirt and dungarees. After 30 miles of scorched earth, the youth said to the trucker, "Well, aren't you going to ask me?" "Ask you what?" drawls the trucker. "If I'm a boy or a girl," answers the youth. "Don't matter none to me," says the trucker, "I'm going to shag you anyhow!"

****

A little boy starts to notice the loud, heavy bouncing noises of his parents having sex at night. Curious, he asks his mother what the noises are. She doesn't really want to go into it, so just explains that she bounces on top of his father to help him to stay thin and to make his stomach smaller. "I don't think it's going to work," says the boy. "Why ever not?" asks the mother. "Because every morning after you go to work, Elsie from next door comes over and blows Daddy back up again!'

****

A barman is delighted when a really top bird walks up and calls him over. She's a real stunner and he's feeling lucky already. "I wonder," she begins in a low, sexy voice, "could I speak to the manager, please?" "I'm afraid he's busy right now," the barman says, not wanting to share this one with anybody or to lose the chance of such a top bird. "Perhaps I can help you instead?" he continues. "I'm not really sure," she says cautiously, stroking him gently on the shoulder. "It's quite a personal issue and I'm not sure you're in charge of the situation." "Oh, I'm in charge; I'm in charge," the barman blurts out. "I'm sure I can take care of your problem." "Well," says the woman, as she touches his face gently and begins to stroke his cheek, "it's like this…" and she slides her fingers into his open mouth, sending him into a fit of joy and excitement, "…can you tell the manager…" "Yes! Yes!" the barman is thinking, "… can you tell the manager there's no toilet paper left in the ladies'?"

****

Two men are walking home from work one hot, sweaty Friday in London. The first man says, "First thing I'm going to do when I get home is rip my wife's knickers off!" "Steady on, mate," says the second. "You've got the whole weekend: why are you in such a hurry?" The first man replies, "They've been chafing my groin all day!"

****

A couple of OAPs – a man and a woman – are sitting outside their old folks' home talking of the old days. All of a sudden an ice cream van pulls up at the gate with the tune playing. The woman says, "I'd love an ice cream, you know," to which the man replies, "Would you like me to get you one?" "Don't bother," the old dear says, "by the time you get to the van you'll never remember what I wanted anyway." "Don't be silly," says the man, "I won't forget. Now, come on: what do you want?" "Well, OK, then," says the woman, "I'll have a double-scoop of strawberry with chocolate sauce, nuts and a flake on top." "A double-scoop of strawberry with chocolate sauce, nuts and a flake on top coming right up," says the man and off he goes. Five minutes later he comes back carrying four hot dogs and two large Cokes. "Oh, my God," says the woman, "I knew I shouldn't have trusted you – where's the gravy?"

****

A man is talking in his favourite bar with his favourite friends on a Sunday night. He says, "So, check this out – last night when I was down here with you lot, a bloody burglar broke into my house." "Well out of order," says his mate. "Did he get anything?" says another. "Yup," says the man, "a smack in the face, a kick up the arse, a plank in the nuts and a dinner-plate over his head – the missus thought it was me coming home pissed again!'

****

A guy breaks down while driving through Wales. Luckily, a farmer stops and offers him a lift to the nearest town, only about 20 miles away. They set off, and after a few minutes they pass by a field full of sheep. All of a sudden the farmer slams on the brakes and leaps out of the van. He hops over the fence, grabs a sheep, sticks its head in the fence and begins to hump it from behind. The guy jumps out and walks up to the fence. "What the hell are you doing?" he asks the farmer. "What the hell does it look like? Why: do you want some?" moans the farmer. "Sure do," says the guy, "but not if you're going to do that with my head."

****

A funeral service is being held for a woman who has recently died. Right at the end of the service the bearers pick up the coffin and begin to carry it to where it will enter the cremation chamber. As they turn a corner in the chapel the coffin hits the wall and there is a loud, audible "OUCH!" from inside it. They drop the casket to the floor and it turns out that, wonder of all wonders, the woman is actually alive. The woman lives for two more years and then dies – presumably for real this time. Everyone goes through the same ceremony, but this time, as the bearers round the corner, the woman's husband shouts out, "Careful, you lot: watch out for the wall!"

****

A man was on a blind date. He had spent the whole evening with this woman he just couldn't stand: she was everything he didn't like in a woman, so he was really bored to death. Luckily he had prepared for just this eventuality and had asked one of his mates to call the restaurant he was eating at, just in case he needed a getaway plan. So when the call came, he rushed over to the phone and feigned surprise and shock. When he returned to the table, his date looked up and asked, "Is everything all right?" He replied, "Not really. I'm afraid I'm going to have to go: my grandfather just died." "Thank God for that," the woman said. "If yours hadn't, mine would have had to!"

****

Jolly Good Sport

Jokes with
balls

After a two-year study, the National Association for Sports and Activities announced the following results on the USA's recreational preferences:

1. The sport of choice for unemployed or imprisoned people is basketball.
2. The sport of choice for maintenance-level employees is bowling.
3. The sport of choice for blue-collar workers is football.
4. The sport of choice for supervisors is baseball.
5. The sport of choice for middle management is tennis.
6. The sport of choice for corporate officers is golf.

Conclusion: The higher you rise in the corporate structure, the smaller your balls!

****

Tiger Woods was having a quiet holiday far away from the sport paparazzi, driving around North Wales in his Volvo. One evening, noticing that he is almost out of petrol, he stopped at a station to fill up. An old man came out from behind an antiquated counter and approached the car. "Fill her up," Tiger Woods said, getting out of the car to stretch his legs. As he did so, a tee fell from his pocket and landed at the feet of the old timer. The petrol attendant picked it up, turned it around in his hands, obviously puzzled, for a full minute. Then, defeated, not able to figure out what it was, he turned to Tiger Woods and asked: "Say, what is this, young man?" "Oh, this is called a tee," the champion golfer answered. Seeing the lack of comprehension in the old timer's eyes, he elaborated: "It's to rest my balls on when I am taking long drives." The man looked him up, then at his car and said admiringly: "They really think of everything at Volvo."

****

Albert Einstein arrives at a party and introduces himself to the first person he sees and asks, "What is your IQ?" to which the man answers: "241." "That is wonderful!" cries Albert in delight. "We shall talk about the Grand Unification Theory and the mystery of the missing mass." The next person Albert introduces himself to is a woman and he asks her: "What is your IQ?" To which the lady answers, "144." "That is great!" responds Albert, very pleased with this party indeed. "We can discuss politics and current affairs. We will have much to discuss!" Albert goes to another person and asks, "What is your IQ?" to which the man answers, "51." Albert responds, "Spurs are doing well this season aren't they?"

****

Two friends are playing golf together, when the first woman swings a mighty shot... that goes up, and up, and down, smack amid a male foursome playing on the next hole. The women watch in horror as the ball actually hits one of the guys, apparently in a most delicate place. They are powerless as they witness the man yelping in pain, both his hands on his crotch and collapsing in a foetal position on the grass. The woman, guilty of the disastrous swing, rushes to meet the foursome and says to the guy in agony on the grass: "Listen I can help. I am an occupational therapist. I can ease your pain, trust me." "I am alright," the bloke says between clenched teeth. "Come on, I can really help." The man agrees and manages to stand up. The occupational therapist then gently unzips his trousers and reaches inside to massage him. "Now?… Are you feeling better now?" "Yeah," the man admits, "that's great, but my thumb still hurts like hell!"

****

A man has been on a desert island for five years. One day, while he was knee deep in the the sea spearing a fish, he notices a strange movement in the water. A few minutes later, a few feet away from him, a gorgeous woman in a tight wet suit stands up. Dumbfounded, he simply watches her approaching, dripping with water, teeth flashing, hips swaying. "How long has it been since you last had a cigarette," she asked in a throaty voice. "Man, it's been ages," the guy answers in a shaky voice. The woman diver opens the zip of her breast pocket and fishes out a packet of cigaretes and a lighter. She places a cigarette in his mouth and lights it. She lets the guy take a drag and then asks: "How long has it been since you last had a nice scotch?" "A long, long time," the guy replies, holding his breath. The woman pulls down the front zip of her wet suit, just enough to reach down and bring out a bottle of bourbon. She places her hands around the neck and gently twists the cap open. She takes a swig, licks the liquid on her lips and passes the bottle to the guy and then asks, her finger toying suggestively with her front zip, "Tell me, how long has it been since you last played around?" "Oh my God," breathes the guy. "Don't tell me you have golf clubs in there, too…"

****

A beautiful young woman is trying out skiing. By the fourth day, she feels confident enough to take the lift with her husband to the top of a gentle slope. While on the lift, stress takes its toll and the desire to visit the bathroom builds up, until it becomes unbearable. Unfortunately, on top of the slope, there is nothing as far as powder rooms go, so the husband, seeing that she desperately needs to go, suggests that she just uses the nearby thicket to do her business: her all-white suit would provide adequate camouflage. The woman weighs her options and realizes that this is the only solution she has if she doesn't want to pee in her suit, so off she goes. The woman is quite a novice at skiing, however, and doesn't really know the position to leave her skis in and, slowly, inexorably, starts sliding down the slope. Gathering speed, she somehow manages to stay on her skis, her bottom bare and her undies wrapped around her ankles. "And this is what happened, doctor," a young man, laying on a hospital bed said to the surgeon. "I was on the lift when I saw this gorgeous woman sliding backwards, half naked and her pants around her ankles. I bent over to get a better view and I fell off the seat and broke my leg." "I see," the surgeon said. "But tell me, how did you break your arm?"

****

Two guys are trying to get in a quick 18 holes, but there are two terrible lady golfers in front of them hitting the ball everywhere but where it's supposed to go. The first guy says, "Why don't you go over and ask if we can play through?" The second guy gets about halfway there, stops and comes back. The first guy says, "What's wrong?" His friend says: "One of these two women is my wife and the other one is my mistress. There is no way I could be seen with both of them! You'll have to go." The first guy laughs: "Yes, I can see that could be a problem! You're right, I'll go over." He gets about halfway there and comes back. The second guy says, "What's wrong?" "Small world," the first guy says with an apologetic grin.

****

A primary school teacher explains to her class that she is a Manchester United fan. She asks the little ones to raise their hands if they are Manchester United fans, too. Not knowing what a Manchester United fan is, but wanting to be liked by their teacher, their hands fly into the air. There is, however, one exception. A little boy named Johnny has not gone along with the crowd. The teacher asks him why he has decided to be different. "Because I'm not a Manchester United fan," he retorts. "Then," asks the teacher, "What are you?" "I'm a proud Arsenal fan!" boasts the little boy. The teacher is a little perturbed now, her face slightly red. She asks Johnny why he is a Gunners fan. "Well, my Dad and Mom are Arsenal fans, so I'm a Arsenal fan, too," he responds. The teacher is now angry. "That's no reason," she says loudly. "What if your Mom was a moron, and your dad was an idiot. What would you be then?" Johnny smiles and says, "Then I'd be a Manchester United fan."

****

A London mortician has a new apprentice who is learning the art of embalming. One day, after a particularly eventful post-match session at Highbury, the cadaver of a Manchester United fan ends up lying on the table of the embalming room. The mortician notes to his apprentice that he is to start the procedure while he finishes filling in a report. The apprentice nods, gathers the tools of his trade and begins examining the body. He rolls it over and, to his amazement, finds a cork in its rectum. Mystified, he pulls it out and immediately hears the "Glory Glory Man United" song come out of the guy's arse. Startled, he shoves the cork back into the cadaver's butt and runs up the stairs to find the mortician: "Sir, you've got to come down and help me, you won't believe what I saw!" Slightly annoyed by the naivety of his assistant, the mortician follows him downstairs. "There, look at the cork in the arse of that body, I couldn't imagine what it was doing there so I pulled it out. You do it." The mortician is a bit surprised to see the cork, too, so he walks to the table and removes it as instructed. The "Glory Glory Man United" song starts playing again out of the dead guy's arse. Sighing, he replaces the cork in its appointed position, turns to his assistant and says: "What's so surprising about that? I've heard thousands of arseholes sing that song."

****

Moses and Jesus were part of a threesome playing golf one day. Moses stepped up to the tee and hit a long drive. The ball landed on the fairway, but rolled directly towards a water hazard. Quickly Moses raised his club, the water parted and the ball rolled to the other side, safe and sound. Next, Jesus strolled up to the tee and hit a nice long drive directly towards the same water hazard. It landed right in the centre of the pond and kind of hovered over the water. Jesus casually walked out on the pond and chipped the ball right up onto the green. The third guy got up and sort of randomly whacked the ball. It headed out over the fence and into oncoming traffic on a nearby street. It bounced off a truck and hit a tree. From there, it bounced onto the roof of a shack close by and rolled down into the gutter, down the drainspout, out onto the fairway and straight towards the pond. On the way to the pond, the ball hit a little stone and bounced out over the water and onto a lily pad, where it rested quietly. Suddenly, a very large bullfrog jumped up on a lily pad and snatched the ball into his mouth. Just then, an eagle swooped down and grabbed the frog and flew away. As they passed over the green, the frog squealed with fright and dropped the ball, which bounced right into the hole for a beautiful hole in one. Moses turned to Jesus and said: "I hate playing with your Dad."

****

Three convicts were on their way to prison. Each had been allowed to take one item with them to help them occupy their time while behind bars. On the bus, one turned to another and said, "So, what did you bring?" The second convict pulled out a box of water paints. "I am going to learn painting. I will produce masterpieces and get filthy rich," he says. Then he asked the first fellow: "What did you bring?" The first convict pulled out a deck of cards and grinned and said: "I brought cards. I can play poker, solitaire and gin, and any number of games. I'll get filthy rich in jail." They both turned to the last convict, quietly sitting by himself, grinning insanely. "Why are you so smug?" the others asked. "What did you bring?" The guy pulled out a box of tampons and said: "I brought these." The other two were – understandably – puzzled. "What can you do with those?" The guy winked and said, pointing to the box: "Well according to this, I can go horse riding, swimming, roller-skating…"

****

A 75-year-old golfer comes back home after a game. "How was your golf game, dear?" asked his wife. "Well, I was hitting the ball pretty well, but my eyesight's gotten so bad I couldn't see where it went," the man said, sounding dejected. "You are 75 years old, Jack," said his wife gently. "I'll tell you what: why don't you take my brother Scott along?" "But he's 85 and doesn't even play golf anymore," protested Jack. "Yes, but he's got perfect eyesight. He could watch your ball for you," Tracy pointed out. The next day Jack teed off with Scott looking on. Jack swung, and the ball disappeared down the middle of the fairway. "Do you see it?" asked Jack. "Yup," Scott answered. "Well, where is it?" yelled Jack, peering off into the distance. "I forgot."

****

A woman had been driving 16 hours straight when she decided she'd had enough: she was still at least six hours away from her destination, it was almost seven o'clock in the morning and she had dozed off and nearly crashed into a telegraph pole. She decided to pull on to a side road and rest for a bit before carrying on. She turned off the car and closed her eyes... drifting off to sleep, precious sleep... All of a sudden an old man in a bright blue jogging suit knocked on her window, scaring her half to death. "Sorry to wake you," he huffed, jogging in place. "But can you tell me what time it is?" The woman glanced at her watch. "7:15," she said through the glass. "Thank you," the jogger said, and left. "Just my luck," the woman muttered angrily. "I'm parked on someone's jogging route." She considered driving off and parking somewhere else, but she was too tired, so she settled back into the seat, trying to re-capture the beautiful dream she was having... Suddenly another jogger knocked on her window. "Hi, do you have the time?" he said. The woman sighed and looked at her watch. "7:19," she said. "Thanks," the jogger said, then trotted off. She looked down the road and saw more joggers coming her way. Irritated, she retrieved a pen from the glove box and scrawled "I DO NOT KNOW THE TIME" on the back of a magazine. She jammed the hastily-constructed sign in the window with her shoulder and settled back to sleep. A jogger knocked on the window just as she started dozing off. The woman pointed at the sign and shouted, "Can't you read?" "Sure I can, ma'am. I just wanted to let you know: it's 7:27."

****

A guy is having a quiet breakfast when he is suddenly interrupted by his wife, who starts yelling at him: "I found this piece of paper in your pocket! Who is Marylou?" "Oh, that's nothing dear," the bloke says. "It's a horse. I bet on this horse last week you see." His wife smiles contritely, realizes she's made a fool of herself and lets it go at that. The bloke goes to work and when he comes back home, he finds his wife on the porch, her face like a thundercloud, having made a mess of his stereo and his collection of CDs on the front lawn. "What is the matter, honey?" he asks. "You got a call from the horse."

****

The Game Warden, fresh out of school, spots a man walking on the bank of the lake carrying two fish in a bucket. "Can I see your fishing licence, sir," he asks. "I did not catch these fish," the fisherman says. "They are my pets. Everyday I come down to the water and whistle and these fish jump out and I take them around to see the sights only to return them at the end of the day." "I do not believe it… You know it is illegal to fish without a licence." "If you don't believe me, then watch," the guy says as he throws the fish back into the water. "Now whistle to your fish and show me that they will come out of the water," the warden says in an ironic tone, to which the man replies: "Fish? What fish?"

****

Topical &
Politics

Jokes for
members

What do Bill Clinton and his dog have in common?
Neither can stop chasing pussy.

What do you call something that's 12 inches long and hangs in front of an arsehole?
A politician's tie!

****

Little Johnny comes home from primary school one day and tells his parents all about the history of St Valentine and Valentine's Day because he has just learned all about it at school. When he has finished, Johnny says to his Mum and Dad, "So I'd really like to send someone very special a Valentine. Do you think that would be OK Mummy. Would it Daddy?" His parents are touched and nod their agreement. "Who is it that you want to give a Valentine's card to Johnny?" asks his father. "Osama Bin Laden," says Johnny. His father is a bit taken aback, and asks why. "Well, Daddy, I thought that if a little American boy like me sends such a nasty man as him a Valentine, he might start to think that the world wasn't really all that bad and that love could conquer all and that he'd spend his time travelling around the world telling people to love instead of hate." "Johnny, that's just beautiful," both of Johnny's parents chime in at the same time. "I know," Johnny says, "and when he's out in the open, the Marines can blow the living crap out of him!"

****

The US President's wife goes to her doctor for a check-up. Her doctor examines her all over, and to his shock, discovers that she has crabs! He begins to panic – how the hell is he going to tell the First Lady she's got a venereal disease? He thinks for a while as she gets dressed and decides he's going to have to beat about the bush. The First Lady sits on the bed, waiting to hear that she's fine. The doctor says, "I'm afraid, ma'am, that you're suffering from rather a strange disease." "Oh, my goodness," she says. "You've got to tell me: what is it?" "Well..." begins the doctor, "it's called... Nixon's Disease." "Oh, my goodness', she says again, "what on earth is that all about? "Well," says the doc, "to put it bluntly, you've got bugs in your Oval Office!"

****

A man on holiday is walking along a beach in the Middle East. He's just strolling around, wearing only a pair of cut-off jeans and sandals. He kicks out at a bottle and is surprised to hear it squeak. He picks the bottle up, pulls out the cork and, funnily enough, a genie appears. "Thank you, O Great One," says the genie. "For freeing me, I will grant you one wish: what will it be?" The man thinks for a while, and then says, "I would like you to bring peace to all of the troubled peoples of this turbulent part of the world, please." The genie magically produces a map and stares at it for a little while. "Wow, O Great One: indeed you do ask for a difficult wish. The peoples of this region have warred long and hard. Warring is part of the fabric that binds the region together. It is not such a simple task – indeed, it is probably the most difficult task you could have come up with for this poor, embarrassed genie. Anything else, O Great One, I will be able to help you with. A million apologies, O Great One." "No problemo," the guy says. "In that case, what I'd like is for my wife to wake me up with a fantastic blowjob tomorrow morning. This will be totally off the top of her head, with no begging or pleading from me – because she wants to give me a blowjob, because she likes it and because it turns her on to see me excited." The genie looks at the guy before turning back to his map and saying, "So, what was that next country called again?"

****

Moral Dilemma: You are in the Middle East with your camera. There have been weeks of rain and there are floods everywhere. You are lucky enough to have survived this huge disaster and you have been able to take some amazing photographs that you have sent to the media back home. One day, you come across Osama Bin Laden holding onto the branch of a tree for dear life – if he lets go he'll be swept away for sure and never be heard from or seen again. You are in a position to help him if you want, but time is tight: you can either reach over and grab his hand to save his life, or you can pick up your camera and snap what will no doubt be remembered as one of the shots of the century... the choice is yours, and the question is... Which lens do you use?!

****

The Gores and the Clintons are flying around the country in Air Force One. All are in a playful mood, so Bill turns to Al and says, "You know what? I could throw a hundred-dollar bill out of the window and I'd make somebody very happy." Al just shrugs his shoulders and says, "I could throw ten ten-dollar bills out of the window and make ten people very happy." Hillary snorts and says, "Well, I could throw one hundred one-dollar bills out of the window and make one hundred people very happy." Chelsea casts her eyes to Heaven and says, "Well, I could throw you all out of the goddam window and cheer up the whole goddam country."

✳✳✳✳

How You Can Tell Your Olympic Event is Fixed:

- The medal ceremony takes place before the event does.
- In the middle of your skating routine, you get hit by someone on skis.
- You see five heads in the four-man bobsled.
- Instead of scores, you hear judges' bribes announced.
- Your event is judged by ITV Digital's accountants.
- You see five judges and a figure skater checking in to a cheap hotel together.

✳✳✳✳

How do you play Taliban bingo?
B-52... F-16... B-1...

What do Osama Bin Laden and Fred Flintstone have in common?
Both may look out their windows and see Rubble.

What is the Afghan national bird?
Duck!

What's the five-day forecast for Afghanistan?
Two days!

What has been the most creative way discussed lately of catching
Osama Bin Laden?
Warplanes spraying Afghanistan with Viagra in the hope that the little
prick will stand up!

****

Osama Bin Laden isn't feeling well and feels that his time in this world is short, so he goes off to consult a psychic in an effort to guage how long he's got left. The woman looks deep into her crystal ball and seems to discover the answer… "You will die… on an American holiday…" she says to him. "An American holiday," says Osama Bin Laden, "but there are many of these. Which American holiday will see my final day?" "That's not really important," says the psychic, "whichever day you die will be an American holiday!"

****

The President's daughter runs into the White House all excited and happy. "Dad," she screams, "You know that Robert guy I've been dating for a year now? Well he's finally asked me to marry him and I've said yes!" "Oh dear, my girl," her dad says, "that's not really going to work. Your mother and I have been married for years, but I have fooled around once or twice you know. That guy Robert is actually your half-brother and you can't really get married to him!" She is broken-hearted, but takes it on the chin and starts seeing guys again. A year later, she comes running back to see her father and says, "Dad! You know that Jim guy I've been dating for a year now? Well he's finally asked me to marry him and I've said yes!" "Oh dear, my girl," he says, "you sure can pick 'em can't you. I'm afraid that he's your half-brother, too!" She is really downhearted and goes to see her mother. "Mom," she says, "I want to get married and every time I do, Dad tells me that I'm related to the man I want to marry!" "Don't pay too much attention to what he says," says her mother. "He's not really your father!"

****

The First Lady goes to see her doctor for a check-up. Her doctor examines her all over, and to her shock, he tells her that she is pregnant! She's in great shape all over, but certainly pregnant. She says that surely there's some kind of mistake, but he assures her, no, there's no mistake and that she is certainly at least three months pregnant. All red and in tears, she storms out of the building and immediately calls up the President on her mobile phone. She gets through to the Oval Office and says she wants to speak to the President right away. The receptionist knows a woman under stress, so puts her straight through. He picks up the phone and hears, "Do you know what you've done to me, you horny bastard? You've gone and got me pregnant, you piece of shit!" The President stays quiet, so the First Lady shouts again, "Do you know what you've done to me, you horny bastard? Answer me!" The President says, "Who is this?"

✱✱✱✱

Late at night in Washington, DC, a well-dressed man is stopped by a masked mugger who sticks a gun in his ribs and says, "If you give me your money and your credit cards you won't get hurt." The man replies, "I'm sorry, I can't do that. I am a Senator. "Well, in that case," the mugger says, "Give me *my* money."

✱✱✱✱

What's the difference between Watergate and Zippergate?
At Zippergate we knew who Deep Throat was.

How will we remember Bill Clinton?
The President after Bush.

What's the difference between Bill Clinton and his dog Buddy?
One's tried to hump the leg of every woman in the White House and the other's a labrador.

What does Bill Clinton say to interns when they leave his office?
Don't bang your head on the desk.

Did you hear about the "Bill Clinton Sale" at the men's outfitters?
All trousers half off.

What's the recipe for Bill Clinton stew?
A small sausage in hot water.

What's the recipe for the new, improved Bill Clinton stew?
One small sausage, a tongue, one cooked goose, a lot of spilled beans and hot water.

What do Monica Lewinsky and the Buffalo Bills have in common?
They both blew the big one several times.

What was the first thing Monica Lewinsky saw in government?
The Executive Branch.

What do Monica Lewinsky and soda machines have in common?
They both have slots which say "Insert Bill Here".

What's the difference between Monica Lewinsky and all the other Americans?
If they want to get some dick in the White House they have to go out and vote.

What did Bill Clinton say when he asked if he had used protection?
Sure, there was a guard standing outside the door.

What's the difference between Bill Clinton and a screwdriver?
A screwdriver turns in screws, whereas Bill Clinton screws interns.

How do you know Bill Clinton is done having sex?
You have to wipe your shirt clean!

****

George W. Bush is out on the town looking for a prostitute. He finds three of them in a bar: a blonde, a brunette and a redhead. He walks up to the blonde and says, "I am a rich man and one of the most powerful men in the world. How much will it cost me to spend some time with you?" The blonde replies, "For you, big guy, it'll cost just $500." He walks up to the redhead and says, "I am a rich man and one of the most powerful men in the world. How much will it cost me to spend some time with you?" The redhead replies, "For you, big boy, it'll cost just $1,000." So George walks up to the brunette and says, "I am a rich man and one of the most powerful men in the world. How much will it cost me to spend some time with you?" The brunette turns to him and says, "Mr President, if you can raise my skirt up as high as you've raised taxes, can get your trousers as low as my wages, can get that thing of yours as hard as times are now, and if you can screw me as well as you've screwed the general public, then baby, it won't cost you a thing!"

****

A famous American magician with a beautiful wife is touring in England. His last show is in London and his shows always end the same way: he asks if any members of the audience have any tricks they would like to perform. On this night, the guy asks the question and someone in the front row shoots his hand into the air. He brings him up on stage and asks him to perform the trick. "Well, I'll need an assistant please," the man says, so the magician brings his beautiful wife out from backstage. The man walks over to the beautiful wife, bends her over, lifts up her skirt and starts shagging her from behind. The magician is taken aback somewhat and pauses for a couple of seconds before saying, "Hey, what the hell are you up to? That's no trick!" And the man replies, "I know, but it's fuckin' magic!"

****

A farmer is working in the fields one day when a huge carload of the Government's Cabinet ministers roar by at one hundred miles an hour. They spin off the road on a really tight bend and end up, upside down, in a ditch. A little bit later a policeman pulls up and asks the farmer if he's seen a car full of Cabinet ministers. The farmer says that he has. "Where are they now then?" Asks the policeman and the farmer replies, "Over there," and points to the ditch, which has been filled in with fresh earth. "You've buried them already?" asks the policeman, "and were they dead?" he continues. The farmer says, "Well… they said they were, but you know how much that lot tell the truth!"

****

The Democrats in the USA announced recently that they are going to change their symbol from a donkey to a condom because the condom more clearly reflects their party's political stance. A condom stands up to inflation, halts production, discourages co-operation, protects a whole load of dicks and gives people a sense of security while screwing others.

****

What do politicians and nappies have in common?
They both need to be changed regularly, and for the same reason.

Why are parliamentarians like self-amusers?
They are both mass debaters.

Why don't prostitutes vote at elections?
They don't care who gets in, so long as somebody loses their deposit.

****